African Literature Today

A review
Edited by Eldred Durosimi Jones

Number 9: Africa, America &
the Caribbean

JC JAMES CURREY

First published by Heinemann Educational Books 1978
Reprinted 1981

First published in the United States of America 1978
by Africana Publishing Corporation

James Currey, Woodbridge, Suffolk

ISBN 978 0 85255 509 5

Transferred to digital printing

James Currey is an imprint of Boydell & Brewer Ltd
PO Box 9, Woodbridge, Suffolk IP12 3DF, UK
and of Boydell & Brewer Inc.
668 Mt. Hope Avenue, Rochester NY 14620, USA
website: www.boydellandbrewer.com

This publication is printed on acid-free paper

Contents

Reviews

Editorial

Alex Haley's *Roots* has suddenly dramatized the realization in fact of the mental yearnings of West Atlantic blacks for a tangible link with their African past. Not that there could have been much doubt about the links, but such was the massive pressure of the 'great Western world' in its material manifestations that, despite the known survivals of Africa in the West Atlantic, in the language, music, dance, religion, and ritual, doubts and uncertainties sometimes seemed to undermine any confidence that such links offer. The practical help that Africa could give downtrodden and beleaguered blacks, at a time when Africa itself in the eyes of European decendants was a place of darkness, must at times – and understandably – have seemed dubious.

One of the great transformations of modern times, starting slowly in the early years of this century, gaining impetus through the Harlem Renaissance, and greatly accelerating since the independence of Ghana, has been the pride with which blacks all over the world now look back on their African origins. Haley beat his way every mile back to his real home and, what is more, the culture in Africa still remembered and recognized the long-exiled son even in his American disguise.

Haley's journey realized in actual geography the leap which Senghor had made in imagination when, encountering American Negro troops in Europe, even in their American war gear, he soon heard the roar of the rivers of Africa:

> Under your closed faces I did not recognize you.
> I only touched the warmth of your brown hand. I said my name 'Africa!'
> And found again lost laughter, I greeted the ancient voice and the roar
> of the cascades of the Congo.

(*Selected Poems*, tr. Clive Reed and John Wake, OUP, 1964)

For many blacks from America, from the Caribbean, from South America, from Britain and the continent of Europe, and even as far away as Australasia, FESTAC '77 was a great collective journey back home, and a great and joyous emotional release, not in as pinpointed a fashion as Alex Haley's, but as proud a return, nevertheless, as Scandinavian Americans and Polish Americans make to their original homelands.

The black man's alienation, particularly in the United States of America, necessitated a search for roots – overtly or covertly. Harlem was a home; it provided some roots, and such were the grinding preoccupations of life there that it would seem to suffice as a total environment. Yet the need was there, and at least in imagination many blacks made the pilgrimage back. This kind of return may be too easily dismissed as sentimental. For those who needed it, it was much more. Ethiopia (from which in physical terms few trans-Atlantic blacks would have originated) became a symbol of home and a source of spiritual satisfaction for many, both in the US and in the Caribbean.

Chester Himes knew of this Africa but it was not his main concern. For him there was no escape from the reality of America; Africa did not exist for him as an alternative. His preoccupation was the Negro revolution at home – the new home. How total and all-preoccupying (and inconvenient) the American environment could be is seen from his scant look past its boundaries to the Africa beyond. The only way out for him was violence there in America. But Africa certainly was a dominant influence in the work of many black writers in North and South America, as well as in the Caribbean.

America too has had its complementary influence on the writing of Africans in Africa. True, the black predicament, the black situation in the New World, was not as fundamental or as dominant an influence on Africans' thinking. Not that African writers ever forgot the great unwilling mass trans-shipment (now sometimes politely called an 'emigration') which took place from their shores through the Atlantic slave trade.

In *A Dance of the Forests*, Wole Soyinka gives an uncomfortable glimpse of an African slave trader selling his brothers down the river at home. Ayi Kwei Armah's slaves (in *Two Thousand Seasons*) never reached America; they escaped and concentrated on reforming their own homeland. Very seldom do African writers treat of the trans-Atlantic slave trade much beyond the limits of their territorial waters, but they often picture the slaves at a later stage in their history, particularly when, crossing the Atlantic themselves in freedom, they re-encounter their brothers in their new home.

J. P. Clark, in *America, Their America*, found them an oasis in an environment which he otherwise found hostile and even threatening. For Senghor the hard pavements of Harlem sprouted green corn to rescue the mind from the steel and concrete oppressiveness of Manhattan.

There were returns too. In Ama Ata Aidoo's *Dilemma Of A Ghost*, Ato complicates the Ghanaian scene by bringing Eulalie, whose thrill at returning 'home' is chilled by blank uncomprehending stares at her dress, language, and manners, until a common human link – motherhood or its frustration – effects a bridge between her and her ancestral cousins. Joe

viii

Golder makes the journey back in Soyinka's *Interpreters* and masochistically attacks his own complexion in an attempt to burn out the white element in his ancestry which his black pride now makes embarrassing. Half-white, half-man, and wretched, his baritone rendering of 'Nobody Knows The Trouble I've Seen', echoing the slave songs of the plantations, portrays both the communal and his personal displacement. His song links the two Atlantic shores.

In a forthcoming article (in *Présence Africaine*), 'The Impact of the New World on Modern African Writing', Dr Sam Asein has traced the influence of black American writers on black South African writers, particularly Mphahlele and Peter Abrahams. One of these inspirers, Langston Hughes, edited, in 1960, one of the earliest of anthologies of modern African writing, *An African Treasury*. The currents have flowed both ways across the Atlantic, and both banks have been enriched by them.

ARTICLES

The African Heritage and the Harlem Renaissance

A Re-evaluation

Lloyd W. Brown

In the past critics have dismissed some African themes in earlier Afro-American literature as mere sentimental primitivism, with the so-called Harlem Renaissance bearing the main brunt of this attack. Stephen H. Bronz, for example, dismisses what he calls the 'artificial tradition' of Africanist themes in Harlem Renaissance writing; according to Wayne Cooper, black writers of the twenties merely perpetuated plantation images of the happy 'primitive Negro'; Sterling Brown alleges that their idealization of Africa 'was more poetic dreaming than understanding'; Harold Isaacs sneers at 'the poet-aesthetes of Harlem ... trooping back to the Kraals and the jungle dens'; and Langston Hughes, who started his writing career in the Harlem Renaissance, is singled out by Arthur P. Davis for a 'phony ... black nationalism' based on 'fantasies' about Africa.[1] These charges have important implications for the black writer's relationship with whatever the writer perceives as cultural roots. How artificial or real are the writer's images of the African past, the rural American South, or the North American ghetto? In using allegorical myths to project images of African and Afro-American sources, do these writers confuse the mythic symbol with the geophysical or socio-economic realities? Does the mythic symbol necessarily reproduce the European's tradition of the 'noble savage'? Or is it a well thought-out, carefully designed expression of those psychological realities which are inherent in the relationship between the writers and their cultural roots?

It is an easy, even obvious, exercise to document the negative criticisms on the basis of some of the more forgettable writers of the Harlem Renaissance. But in dealing with a pan-Africanist tradition in the period as a whole we need to look carefully at its precise implications in the works of the more significant writers. These implications are not limited to the

I

Harlem Renaissance of course; the Negritude writers in both Africa and the Caribbean have been repeatedly accused of a sentimental idealism in their conception of an African heritage, and in more recent times black nationalist writers in the United States have not always avoided lapses into a banal exoticism. But I have chosen to concentrate on the Renaissance group for three reasons. First, in their case the allegations of sentimentality and distortion have largely gone unanswered – have even been tacitly accepted – while major Negritude writers like Senghor and Césaire have always (and deservedly so) had their defenders against wrong-headed interpretations.[2] Secondly, on the *surface* at any rate, the writers with whom I am dealing at length here (Claude McKay, Countee Cullen, and Langston Hughes) seem to justify the usual allegations. By contrast, this problem, or apparent problem, does not really arise in any substantial way with prominent black nationalist writers in our own time, since in their works the Afro-American's cultural revolution relies very little, if at all, on a carefully sustained structure of African symbols. Amiri Baraka (LeRoi Jones), for example, does not really devote much time or space to an African heritage as such in his more frankly revolutionist writings where it is the black ghetto, more often than not, that functions as a symbolic cultural source. In the English-speaking Caribbean Derek Walcott obviously obviates charges of sentimental exoticism by virtue of his sustained, no-nonsense emphasis on the very real gulfs between the West Indies and Africa, or between West Indian dreams of an undiluted African heritage, on the one hand, and on the other hand, the hybrid nature of the West Indian's culture. And Walcott's contemporary, Edward Brathwaite, handles Akan materials in his *Masks* with an authoritative touch that has actually won him praise in some quarters for his *African* realism.[3]

However, when we turn to the Harlem Renaissance, it is tempting at first glance to place the black *bon vivants* of Claude McKay's fiction within the 'noble savage' tradition, and to argue that McKay and his contemporaries sentimentalize the poor black and the African past because of guilt about their Western, middle-class status, in much the same way that the guilt-ridden complexes of Rousseau's slave-trading Europe found expression in the original images of the noble savage. But I would suggest that in dealing with cultural images and pan-Africanist symbols in major Harlem Renaissance writers we need to go beyond this first glance, beyond superficial impression to a careful consideration of the significance of the African past in these writers.

This brings me to my third point. The Harlem Renaissance writers experience a special, though not unique, relationship with the rhetoric and substance of their African themes, a relationship that is largely due to the mood of the period itself. This is not by way of accepting the very notion of a 'Renaissance' as such, with its invidious and persistent implications of a prolonged cultural slumber during the two centuries before the twenties. That notion of a sudden beginning or rebirth distorts and actually negates the essential continuity of the *Afro-American* heritage of the 'Renaissance' writers themselves, however neatly it may fit in with the schematic divisions which always seem necessary to the literary historian. The really important question about the Harlem Renaissance as renaissance, and one which is crucial to their perception of their own African themes, is the extent to which the intellectuals of the period fostered the *idea* of a rebirth or awakening. Alain Locke's image of a 'new Negro' may very well represent a shallow and distorting perception of black American history and culture as a dynamic continuum, but in so far as that idea shapes the self-awareness and literary insights of the period, then it remains a reality to be reckoned with.[4] And one area on which this reality impinges is the imaginative vision of Africa.

On the whole there is a marked self-consciousness in that vision. In lesser hands it becomes a ludicrous self-indulgence. But at best that self-conscious preoccupation with the African heritage, and with the black past in general, stems from the period's conviction about its pioneering role. On the one hand there is a felt need to explore their heritage, and on the other hand, there is the fear, or assumption, that such a heritage is elusive at best. The point is not that the Renaissance writers were ignorant of a black past: the anthologies of the period offer ample proof to the contrary. But the literary exploration of the past is self-consciously tentative because of a prevailing sense, detectable in the tone of the works, that this kind of thing is really a new undertaking – a new problem for the black artistic imagination and for a collective black psyche. In short, their relationship with their African themes is rooted in a sense of distance which is heightened by the fact that Africa was, quite simply, far less accessible, in every sense, to black America of the twenties than it is in the seventies. They therefore undertake their African themes as self-appointed pioneers in a period in which first-hand knowledge of Africa was rare; and precisely because of these reasons their pan-African themes are fraught with ambiguities which are significant in the role of cultural roots in the black experience.

On this basis, Claude McKay's *Home to Harlem* exists in a more complex relationship with the 'noble savage' tradition than has usually been assumed. Of course the novel does not concern itself at length with an African heritage as such, but it does explore the question of cultural roots (represented here by Harlem) in terms which shed considerable light on the African motifs in his poetry and that of his contemporaries. First, it is important to note that the sentimental expectations and nostalgic idealism with which Jake returns to Harlem (from Europe) are specifically attributed to Jake's homesickness and they do not exist in the novel as an authoritative point of view. Secondly, when Jake's rough-and-tumble experiences in Harlem remind him of the total realities of life in the ghetto, he realizes that Harlem can be just as brutish, in some regards, as the white Americans who have brutalized the black community. This eventual disillusionment implies a pointed rejection of the earlier sentimentalization of Harlem. Raymond, the Haitian *émigré* whose Caribbean background is a reminder of McKay's Jamaican nationality, is similar to Jake in this regard, though on a more sophisticated level. Hence, whatever romantic or sentimental images of Harlem appear in the novel, they are the considered projections of Raymond's (and McKay's) cultural longings: first, as West Indians they sentimentalize Harlem because they are projecting their nostalgia and homesickness on it and, secondly, this nostalgia is integral to that broader and deeper longing, shared by black middle-class intellectuals, for experiences (including the African past) which are removed from their immediate ambience and which, for that very reason, assume idyllic proportions. And, finally, as in Jake's case, Raymond's final perception of Harlem implies a critical awareness of his sentimental idealism: he is aware not only of Harlem's vibrance, but also of its brutality.

To sum up, McKay is not merely reproducing or succumbing to sentimental notions of the 'noble savage' in the black imagination. He is actually examining its causes and its effects, and this examination becomes a deliberate self-analysis of black intellectuals like McKay himself. When Raymond admits his loathing for the brutalizing realities of black poverty he is also acknowledging the actual source of his sentimental idealism: it reflects his expatriation from his Caribbean roots (and of all black middle-class intellectuals from what they perceive as their African or Afro-Western heritage), and it is therefore a guilty attempt to compensate for his feelings of incompatibility with that lost world. The fundamental issue in the novel is not Harlem as such, but the emotional and intellectual experience of coming 'home' to the cultural origins which we associate with Harlem, the Caribbean, or the African past. McKay's object is to examine the nostalgia of all uprooted blacks and, more incisively, of black intellectuals like Raymond. Raymond is the victim of the conflicts and sentimental obsessions that are inherent in the search for cultural roots but, even more important, he is also a critical analyst of these very obsessions. And in this regard Raymond's personality embodies the kind of duality that marks his *Harlem Shadows*.[5]

This is essentially the sense of duality in those *Harlem Shadows* poems in which McKay explores the significance of the African past in his Western experience. 'Outcast' is one of his most forthright analyses of that duality. On the one hand, the 'great western world holds me in fee', permanently, but on the other hand, his spirit longs for an African past. There is no sentimental nostalgia here. The poet has no illusion about the possibilities of recapturing that past. Thus the poem's structure is based on a consistent tension between a hard-headed realism about his Western milieu and a firm grasp of the strength, as well as the limits, of his non-Western allegiances. And the ambiguities of his identity are reflected in the multiple meanings of his language. The African 'regions' of the past are now 'dim' or forgotten as a result of an acquired ignorance, because of his place in a Western world which can see Africa only as 'dim' or savagely mysterious. The double connotations of the African image reflect contrasting states of mind in the poet's black self-perception. Similarly, the complaint that his spirit longs for Africa but is 'bondaged' by the body updates the history of physical slavery by emphasizing one of its most enduring effects – that spiritual slavery to which blacks as well as whites are accessories. The admission that the great Western world holds him 'in fee' describes the black complicity in a continuing spiritual bondage; for not only is 'great' a sarcastic salute to the Western world's arrogant self-regard, but it also reflects that allegiance which allows even the rebellious black to feel the pull of the real splendours of Western 'greatness'. This interweaving of Western loyalties and black self-regard is climaxed halfway through the sonnet when the poet sees himself bending his knees to the 'alien gods' of the West.

The acceptance of his Western identity is undeniable here, particularly in that suggestive image of the bended knee: bondage has become a kind of obeisance. But the simultaneous sense of alienation from the West is equally clear in the phrase 'alien gods'. The Westerner's pejorative phrase for non-Christian religions has been turned against the West itself: the semantic gesture confirms both his skills in the Western mode and his detachment from the Western world as a whole. McKay and the West are simultaneously joined together and alienated by each other. And as a consciously hostile alien, rather than an obeisant captive, he perceives himself as a wandering 'ghost', a 'thing apart' who was born 'under the white man's menace, out of time'. The phrase 'out of time' has multiple connotations which, taken together, intensify the theme of isolation from both Africa and the West: he has been born out of 'time' (history), not in the Western sense of an African without history, but in the sense that his Western milieu has cost him an intimacy with that African history that has always existed; in musical terms, his Western-African background has created a conflict, the disharmony which is analogous to being out of (musical) time, but which also has an immediate reference to the poet's wistful longing for a cultural heritage that is enshrined in music ('My soul would sing forgotten jungle songs'); finally, to be 'out of time' is to be out of step, to be isolated from those others who enjoy a tangible heritage and an unbroken sense of history;

but to complete the complex of ambiguous meanings, being isolated is not merely a negative experience but a positive indication of that detachment which is inherent in a searching, uncompromising perception of one's experience. Both in theme and structure, 'Outcast' remains one of the most effective poems by a New World black on the self-conflicts and ambiguities that are intrinsic to being black in the West.

'Africa', on the other hand, represents a calculated attempt to break out of the outcast role in order to look closely at Africa. That scrutiny brings mixed results. It confirms those longings which motivate the assertion of his (non-Western) humanity in 'Outcast', but it also reveals an African past with flaws as well as glories. The poem unfolds in a series of images that enforce a sense of historical degeneration. Africa is transformed in stages from a vital woman ('The sun sought thy dim bed'), mother ('The sciences were suckling at thy breast'), and finally mere harlot whose 'time is done'. Its darkness is, successively, a proud racial emblem, the fertile womb of humane cultures, and the tomb of civilizations that were destroyed by white (*and* African) 'Honour and Glory, Arrogance and Fame'. And the implied complicity of the West in Africa's downfall is reinforced by the parallels between the decline of old African empires in this poem, and the anticipated decline of the West in 'America'. Altogether, the attempt in 'Africa' to perceive Africa and its past in complex rather than simplistically idealistic terms becomes an important commentary on the outcast sensibilities which foster an idyllic vision of Africa in 'Outcast'. In 'Africa' McKay makes explicit that complex, realistic approach to the past which the outcast in the other poem lacks but which – and this is crucial – he admits to losing in 'Outcast'. The poet's distance, in time and space, from Africa is not merely being acknowledged here. It has also become a deliberately chosen basis for exploring his sense of cultural distance from Africa, his filial yearnings for the ethno-cultural substance that Africa seems to promise, and, conversely, his antipathy-attraction to the West. Once again, the *African image* projects the writer's perception of his *Western reality*, and the psycho-cultural ambiguities which flow from that reality.

This is the kind of function which links McKay's African image with the work of Countee Cullen. Thus the latter's poem, 'Heritage', is not merely a reproduction of 'unreal' ideas or 'poetic dreaming' about Africa. More precisely, it is a self-critical inquiry into the nature and function of the African idyll in the black American's consciousness:

> What is Africa to me:
> Copper sun or scarlet sea,
> Jungle star or jungle track,
> Strong bronzed men, or regal black
> Women from whose loins I sprang
> When the birds of Eden sang?[6]

The initial statement suggests both contemptuous indifference or detachment, and an earnest groping for Africa's real significance. But, just as Raymond's loathing of the black lumpenproletariat heightens his guilty idealization of it in *Home to Harlem*, so are the meanings/images of Cullen's Africa attributable to a guilty recognition of that other, more negative, response to Africa. The more obvious self-conflicts of Cullen's themes are well known – the black American's dual allegiance to a black past and a white present, the tension between Christian loyalties and 'pagan' non-Christian longings. But here, too, we need to go beyond the obvious, to examine the symbolical texture of Cullen's poetry. And as far as the quest for cultural roots (in Africa) is concerned, Cullen appears to be (1) acknowledging the idyllic, or 'unreal', nature of the African image in his consciousness, and (2) attributing this sentimental image to the physical and psychological distance which makes Africa inaccessible, and therefore alluringly idyllic. The crucial 'meaning' of the poem does not lie with the actuality of Africa as such, but with the subjective emphasis of the opening query (What does Africa mean to *me*?), and with the very nature of the poet's attempt to establish Africa's meaning. Like McKay, Cullen is primarily concerned with the writer's personal relationship with his rhetorical and mythic materials. What makes 'Heritage' and comparable works by McKay so interesting is that they reproduce certain fantasies about cultural roots, but do so with a self-critical awareness about the nature of their cultural sources and conflicts.

From this it follows that these issues are not only the burden of a collective Afro-Western psyche. On a special and intensified level they are also central to the artistic imagination and role of the writer himself. Hence, in the final analysis, 'Outcast' is not simply an exploration of the perennially divided outcast archetype. It is simultaneously a demonstration of the creative spirit which allows the archetype, but more specifically the artist, to transcend the fragmenting consequences of the outcast role. That most honoured of Western poetic forms, the sonnet, has become McKay's medium for establishing his distance from the dishonour of Western history, and for simultaneously exploring the frank implications of his wishful fantasies about singing 'jungle songs'. In effect, the duality of the poem itself – a Western form adopted, even subverted, for a peculiarly Afro-Western vision – is a self-consciously created artistic form; and as such it is a harmonious structure which signalizes the poet's role in transforming the fragmentation of the outcast's past into a dynamic and essentially integrated kind of dualism.

Langston Hughes's poetry offers some of the most sustained and explicit examples of this transforming power of art (especially poetry, music, and dance).[7] In 'Afro-American Fragment', for example, the fragmentation of the black past is transformed into a harmonious duality by way of the art forms usually associated with the black musician and the black poet:

> So long
> So far away
> Is Africa.
> Not even memories alive
> Save those that history books create,
> Save those that songs
> Beat back into the blood –
> Beat out of blood with words sad-sung
> In strange un-Negro tongue.

Here the black American's African heritage is really experienced as a creative process that should be distinguished from the creations (i.e. fabrications) of history books. Hence black music demonstrates the duality of the black American identity by fusing together disparate materials drawn from the past. An African 'beat' or rhythm is combined with the slavery of the past ('beat out of blood') and with the non-African language and culture of a Western heritage ('strange un-Negro tongue'). In forging a new, hybrid art form, the black musician is therefore an archetypal symbol of his own cultural history in which the transplanted African created an 'Afro-American' identity from the fragments of an African past, the Western present, and the distinctive experience of being black in white America. And, in turn, the musician's re-creation of the 'Afro-American' experience has now been implicitly duplicated by the poet.

From this point of view one may detect a certain kind of subtlety in a poem like 'Danse Africaine'. For the initial impression of a simplistically overwhelming African presence – due to the insistent beating of the tom-toms behind the dancer – is balanced by the pivotal halfway lines of the poem:

> Dance!
> A night-veiled girl
> Whirl softly into a
> Circle of light.

The dancer image combines the symbolism of the spotlight ('white', and a product of Western technology) with the suggestive blackness of the dancer's colour and/or costume ('A night-veiled girl'). It is therefore appropriate that this image occurs at the halfway point in the poem because its metaphoric celebration of a cultural synthesis literally becomes a central pivot for the insistent, and more obtrusive, tom-tom images. The total structure of the poem presents the African tom-tom, not as the escape fantasy of some phony black nationalism, but as an active cultural memory that continues to beat even as it becomes a part of a non-African world. And

8

by extension, the tom-tom's musical re-creation of the Afro-American's cultural history is being duplicated by the harmonious duality of the poet's own art. In retrospect, that dancer image does not merely stand at the centre of the poem. It exists at the very heart of an under-rated but crucial literary tradition.

NOTES

1. Stephen H. Bronz, *Roots of Negro Consciousness: The 1920s: Three Harlem Renaissance Authors*, New York, Libra Publishers, 1964, p. 15; Wayne Cooper, 'Claude McKay and the New Negro of the 1920s', *The Black American Writer Volume II: Poetry and Drama*, ed. C. W. E. Bigsby, London, Pelican edition, 1971, p. 61; Sterling Brown, *Negro Poetry and Drama*, New York, Atheneum edition, 1969, p. 75; Harold Isaacs, 'Five Writers and their African Ancestors', *Phylon*, XXI, 3, 1960, p. 244; Arthur P. Davis, 'Langston Hughes: Cool Poet', *College Language Association Journal*, 11, 1967–8, p. 285.
2. But see my paper 'The Expatriate Consciousness in Black American Literature', *Studies in Black Literature*, III, 2, Summer 1972, pp. 9–12.
3. See, for example, Ama Ata Aidoo, 'Akan and English', *West Africa*, 21 September 1968, p. 1099; Maureen Warner-Lewis, 'Odomankoma Kyrema Se', *Caribbean Quarterly*, XIX, 2, June 1973, pp. 51–99.
4. Alain Locke, *The New Negro*, New York, Atheneum edition, 1969.
5. Claude McKay, *Harlem Shadows: The Poems of Claude McKay*, New York, Harcourt, Brace, 1922. See 'Outcast', p. 45, 'Africa', p. 35, and 'America', p. 6.
6. *On These I Stand: An Anthology of the Best Poems of Countee Cullen*, New York, Harper & Row, 1947, p. 24.
7. The Langston Hughes poems discussed here are taken from *Selected Poems of Langston Hughes*, New York, Knopf, 1971, pp. 3, 7.

Through the Looking Glass: African and Irish Nationalist Writing

C. L. Innes

> How in the name of heaven can he escape
> That defiling and disfiguring shape
> The mirror of malicious eyes
> Casts upon his eyes until at last
> He thinks that shape must be his shape?
> (W. B. Yeats, 'Dialogue of Self and Soul')

In 1921, James Weldon Johnson, a leading poet and spokesman for Afro-Americans who participated in the Harlem Renaissance, wrote in his Preface to *The Book of American Negro Poetry*:

> What the colored poet in the United States needs to do is something like what Synge did for the Irish; he needs to find a form which will express the racial spirit by symbols from within rather than by symbols from without, such as the mere mutilation of English spelling and pronunciation . . .[1]

The analogy between Irish and black writing recurs. Alain Locke wrote in 1925 that as a centre for 'folk-expression and self-determination' Harlem had 'the same role to play for the New Negro as Dublin has had for the New Ireland or Prague for the New Czechoslovakia'.[2] Countee Cullen and Padraic Colum met in 1931 and compared notes on the situation of Irish and Negro writers, a meeting recorded in Cullen's 'The Visit'. The Afro-American critic, Sterling Brown, pointed out the similarities between stereotypes of Irish and Negroes,[3] and, more recently, Conor Cruise O'Brien has compared the Sinn Fein and Black Power movements.[4]

That there should have been similarities between the situation and aims of African and Irish writers, and that they should have learned from one another, is not surprising. Both sought to identify with a national or ethnic group and to express the culture and characteristics of that group; both affirmed that culture in reaction to centuries of devaluation and repression. Both groups sought to redefine their groups as a people worthy of self-government, and, to do so, fashioned or revived an appropriate mythology, and created a new kind of language, imagery, form, and style which might speak for and/or to the oppressed group.

What is surprising, however, is the degree to which the national definitions made by writers of the Irish Renaissance, the Harlem Renaissance, the Negritude and Negrismo movements, and the 'Black Arts' movement of the sixties in America, sound similar. All contrast their spirituality, emotional warmth, vitality, and intuitiveness with a mechanistic, artificial, rationalistic, and sterile Anglo-Saxon or European culture. African and Gaelic cultures, the nationalists maintain, are collective, expressive of the people as a whole, most authentic when associated with music and dance and the spoken word. Given the fact that the nationalist seeks to express the uniqueness of his culture as a way of validating the group's drive for independence; given the fact that Yeats strove to recreate a distinctively Irish literature, just as Senghor strove to re-create and define a distinctively African culture; it still seems odd that their formulations should be so similar. One explanation is that Celts and Africans are indeed culturally similar, and in some ways no doubt they are – either as a result of colonial oppression or because their pre-colonial and pre-industrial cultures contained some elements in common. But another and more likely explanation seems to me that both groups are reacting to the same Western myth and are caught up in the same Western dialectic. In other words, the redefinitions of Irish and Africans are similar because the colonial image of Irish and blacks was almost identical.

In *The Wretched of the Earth*, Frantz Fanon describes the psychological structure with which colonialism is rationalized as a Manichean world. Two spheres are established, physically and mentally. Segregation, apartheid, the creation of ghettos are justified and reinforced by this dual vision opposing the idealized society of the colonizer to the demonic state of the 'native'. The settler lives in a clean, well-lit, and well-ordered town; the native's quarters are squalid, dark, and chaotic. The settler is civilized, rational, moral, religious, enlightened; the native is inherently barbarous, irrational, the enemy of morality, superstitious, living in a state of darkness. And as Fanon goes on to say, 'The customs of the colonized people, their traditions, their myths – above all, their myths – are the very sign of that poverty of spirit and their constitutional depravity.'

Even those writers who call imperialism, or perhaps more accurately imperialists, into question, accept the vision of two opposed worlds, though usually in less extreme terms than those described by Fanon. Conrad's *Heart of Darkness*, however critical and however metaphorical, nevertheless rests on the assumption that the truly African world is indeed representative of darkness, the irrational and the primitive and untamed. Joyce Cary's Mister Johnson is not quite reduced to the status of a pet, but is portrayed as a charming, irrational, superstitious, and childlike clown – never, and this is the point, as a man capable of governing himself and his fellow men.

Fanon was describing the structure established by the French in Africa and the Caribbean, but that structure of two opposed worlds is equally applicable to the Englishmen's concept of themselves in relation to the Irish. Thus, in 1868, Benjamin Disraeli wrote in a letter to *The Times*:

> [The Irish] hate our free and fertile isle. They hate our order, our civilization, our enterprising industry, out sustained courage, our decorous liberty, our pure religion. This wild, reckless, indolent, uncertain and superstitious race have no sympathy with the English character. Their fair ideal of human felicity is an alternation of clannish brawls and coarse idolatry. Their history describes an unbroken circle of bigotry and blood.[5]

And a letter from Charles Kingsley to his wife, written while he was touring Ireland in 1860, epitomizes the nineteenth-century Anglo-Saxon attitude towards Britain's subject peoples:

> But I am haunted by the human chimpanzees I saw along that hundred miles of horrible country. I don't believe they are our fault. I believe there are not only more of them than of old, but that they are happier, better, more comfortably fed and lodged under our rule than they ever were. But to see white chimpanzees is dreadful; if they were black, one would not feel it so much, but their skins, except where tanned by exposure, are as white as ours.[5]

The more amiable but nevertheless paternalistic image of the Irish is typified by Matthew Arnold in his lectures advocating a Chair of Celtic Studies at Oxford. In contrast to the honesty, industry, and sense of order which marked the Germanic element in the English, Arnold claimed, the Celt was marked by sentiment, by sensitivity to joy and sorrow; his nature was 'to aspire ardently after life, light, and emotion, to be expansive, adventurous and gay . . . He loves bright colours, easily becomes audacious, over-crowding, full of fanfaronade . . . He is *always ready to react against the despotism of fact*' (Arnold's italics), but lacking 'balance, measure and patience,' is always unsuccessful both in his rebellion and his spiritual creations.[6]

I have quoted Arnold and his compatriots' views at some length because I want to stress the extraordinary similarity between colonial images of Irish and Africans, a similarity which readers acquainted with literature about Africans and 'darkies' will be quick to recognize. Certainly Arnold's description of the Celt could be applied word for word to the black-faced minstrel in the American stage tradition, to Amos and Andy, and to Cary's Mister Johnson. What the similarity indicates, I believe, is the rigidity of the colonizer's conceptual system rather than any actual likeness between the colonized peoples.

But for English and French colonizers and plantation owners it was not enough to nourish and maintain these images in their own minds; the 'supremacy' of the white man, the 'need' of the native must be acknowledged 'loudly and intelligibly'[7] by the colonized themselves. And so, as Fanon puts it in *Black Skin, White Mask*:

> Every colonized people – in other words, every people in whose soul an inferiority complex has been created by the death and burial of its local cultural originality – finds itself face to face with the language of the civilizing nation; that is with the culture of the mother country. The colonized is elevated above his jungle status in proportion to his adoption of the mother country's cultural standards. He becomes whiter as he renounces his blackness, his jungle.[8]

Although Fanon speaks from his experience of the French, whose emphasis on cultural assimilation was in most cases more intense than the British or American, the difference has been one of degree rather than kind, and the effects of such assimilation are satirized not only by Léon Damas and Mongo Beti, but also by LeRoi Jones, Wole Soyinka (e.g. in *The Lion and the Jewel* and *The Interpreters*), and James Joyce.

Even when the colonized writer does acknowledge his identity with his native country and people, he may continue to view both through the colonizer's eyes; he sees them as exotic or idyllic, rather than as part of his everyday world – as the norm. In a 1959 essay the Antillean writer Rene Menil analysed this phenomenon: 'Whence comes this depersonalization and alienation? I see myself as strange and exotic. Why? I am exotic to myself because my perception of myself is the white man's perception which has become my own after three centuries of colonial conditioning.'[9] Menil draws an analogy between the colonizer's viewpoint and that of the theatre audience. To the settler, the native is merely part of the decor, never an actor who has a meaningful part in the drama. Related to the phenomenon of colonial exoticism is the view of the native people and country as symbolic of some psychic state, as in *Heart of Darkness* or O'Neill's *Emperor Jones*. Gilbert Gratiant's poems often represent the Caribbean as an idyllic and innocent world, and Allingham's Irish poems such as 'The Fairies' reinforce the desire to see the inhabitants of Eire as naive and childlike.

To early writers in colonized Ireland, Africa, and the Americas, three options seemed available: the writer could conceal his identity and take pride in his ability to write so skilfully that no critic would guess his origin;

he could write 'as a native', using the stock dialect forms and 'the two main stops, humor and pathos', James Weldon Johnson described as typical of dialect literature;[10] or he could openly protest against the economic and political oppression of his people, using the literary language and forms that had long been sanctioned by the European tradition. The Afro-Americans William Stanley Brathwaite and Paul Lawrence Dunbar (in his early poems) chose the first option, as did the Irish writers Sheridan, Wilde, and Allingham. Dunbar, Gratiant, Claude McKay, and Allingham also chose the second style for their 'folksy' pieces which they regarded as far less significant than their more 'universal' works in the European tradition. As Dunbar wrote towards the end of his life:

> He sang of life, serenely sweet,
> With now and then, a deeper note.
> From some high peak, nigh yet remote,
> He voiced the world's absorbing beat.
>
> He sang of love when earth was young,
> And Love, itself, was in his lays.
> But ah, the world, it turned to praise
> A jingle in a broken tongue.

Finally one can cite the novels of W. E. B. DuBois, or Charles Chesnutt (but not his stories), or Peter Abrahams, or the sonnets of Claude McKay or Gwendolyn Brooks, or the 'Spirit of the Nation' ballads composed by Thomas Davis and his nineteenth-century Irish compatriots, as examples of works committed to political change, but unquestioning in their adherence to Western literary convention.

All too often, these writers failed to come to terms with the fact so clearly demonstrated by Fanon that the colonizer's domination was mental as well as physical, and they accepted unthinkingly the very assumptions of native cultural inferiority which were used by the colonial power to justify its presence. But in the 1890s in Ireland, and later in Africa, the Caribbean, and Afro-America, many intellectuals began to emphasize the need to 'decolonize the mind', and to restore the full humanity of their peoples in their own eyes as well as in the eyes of those who had colonized them. The means for mental decolonization that these writers advocated was cultural nationalism – the restoration and celebration of what they believed to be the authentic culture of the nation.

One of the primary assumptions of cultural nationalism is that the particular national or ethnic group in question has already created and must continue to develop a culture which is radically different from the metropolitan civilization. In affirming such a tradition the intellectuals are also rejecting the absolutism of the colonizer's cultural and aesthetic standards.

At the same time they often assert as a new absolute a set of standards claimed to be expressive of the colonized group. Sartre's formulation of Negritude as an antithesis to the thesis of white supremacy[11] – a formulation to which Senghor later gave his assent – is, I think, applicable to other manifestations of cultural nationalism. But what is striking and paradoxical about the antithesis proclaimed by nationalist intellectuals is the degree to which it derives from and affirms the antithetical images already developed by the colonizer in order to justify his presence. Rather than deny those distinctions and insist the Celt or African is as capable of reason and science as the Anglo-Saxon or Gaul, these intellectuals celebrate the very attributes for which their race was disparaged – emotionalism, irrationality, primitiveness. Despite his warning against letting the enemy plant cabbages in the Irish rose garden, Yeats merely qualifies Arnold's dichotomy between the Anglo-Saxon and the Celt by arguing that the Celtic touch is really a kind of primeval spirituality untainted by English rationality and materialism.

Similarly, Senghor asserted that African culture is essentially emotional rather than rational, intuitive rather than analytical, spiritual rather than materialistic or technological, that 'emotion is completely Negro as reason is Greek'. In the Epilogue to *Ethiopiques* (Paris, 1956), Senghor wrote of what he deemed the definitively African qualities in black poetry: 'Rhythm, the very navel of the poem, is born of emotion, and, in its turn, engenders emotion. And also humour, the other aspect of Negritude.' Rhythm, emotionalism, humour: these are the ingredients of the very minstrel stereotype against which Negritude was intended to do battle. Claude McKay's novels such as *Banjo* (1929) and *Banana Bottom* (1931) also celebrate those characteristics, and particularly in the early stages of the Harlem Renaissance and the Negrismo movement, one finds an acceptance and glorification of the Afro-American as essentially primitive, representative of the *id* as opposed to the repressive Western *super-ego*, Dionysian rather than Apollonian.

Both the African and the Irish view of the nature of their cultures can be seen within the context of two conflicting concepts of history which recur throughout European thought: the one imagines history as evolution and stresses linear progress; the other, typified by the Romantics and Yeats as well as Senghor, imagines history as degeneration from an idealized past and tends to assume a cyclical, often apocalyptic movement towards change. In a colonial situation, the colonizer justifies his presence with the concept of history as evolution; he brings linear progress to a people that has remained 'static', providing an example to the colonizer of what he has evolved from. In contrast, the group struggling for independence tends to see its recent history as degeneration; the pre-colonial past becomes associated with an ideal and unfallen state which is to be restored once the forces of evil and corruption represented by the alien culture are repelled. In the pronouncement of the cultural nationalists, that past, to be found, in Douglas Hyde's words, 'at the bottom of the heart',[12] becomes identified with the poetic, and is contrasted with a metropolitan culture which is seen as essentially prosaic and scientific. The culture of people with 'soul', spiritual and reverent, whose everyday speech and life are seen as vital, rhythmic, rich, and natural, is opposed to the oppressor's supposedly mechanistic, artificial, and sterile culture. The native culture is said to be essentially agrarian, pastoral, innocent; the colonizer contaminates it with a way of life that is urban, materialistic, and corrupt – he is the serpent in the Celtic or African Eden. Such an identification of the native tradition with the poetic implies that to be a poet one need only express the national culture, and Irish and black writers alike tend to blend the search for authentic self-expression, for the pure self 'at the bottom of the heart', with the desire to identify and speak forth the national spirit in its original and uncontaminated form. Aimé Césaire's *Cahier d'un retour au pays natal* is a powerful and rich expression of that inter-related search, and Countee Culleen's 'Heritage' employs the trope which occurs again and again in the literature of the Harlem Renaissance, Negritude, and the Black Arts movement, identifying the pulse of his blood with the pulse of African drums.

Just as the authentic or original self is sought in a purer Edenic past, authentic poetry is, according to the nationalists, to be found in the culture which has been uncontaminated by the metropolitan civilization; that is, in the pre-colonial past or in the folk tradition which has survived colonialism. The intellectual who has been educated by the colonizer seeks for the aesthetic standards, forms, and content of his writings among the uneducated. Langston Hughes took and modified blues and 'shout' forms; Sterling Brown wrote folk ballads often based on legendary folk heroes; James Weldon Johnson's best work draws on the form and content of the folk sermon. In French West Africa, Birago Diop drew on the traditional *griôt* tales; Senghor translated tales and poems from Serer, his native language, and his poetry often seeks to re-create traditional oral forms in their use of assonance and alliteration, musical accompaniment, rhythm, and declamatory style. Caribbean poets developed 'tam-tam' rhythmic forms, or imitated the beat and movement of Afro-Cuban dance. Nicolas Guillén's use of the *son* is expressive of his desire to identify with the popular tradition in Cuba. Ireland calls to mind Yeats tramping around the Coole Park estate with Lady Gregory while the tenants foraged for tales to please their landlady. Other manifestations include Douglas Hyde's Gaelic songs and plays, Synge's visits to the Aran Islands, and the collections of legends rendered by Standish O'Grady and Lady Gregory, providing the source for the many plays based on the story of Deidre and the Cuchulain cycle.

The search for authenticity in 'the folk' is not, of course, limited to cultural nationalism. As Raymond Williams has demonstrated in great detail in *The Country and the City* (New York, 1973), the idealization of the country and the investment in it of the virtues of community and authenticity become increasingly apparent in English and European literature as the impact of the Industrial Revolution is felt by intellectuals. In turning to the peasant to represent the elemental feelings in purer and more vital form than the urban dweller, Wordsworth and Synge are part of the same tradition. Yet however much Synge, Senghor, or Cullen might be influenced by the pastoral tradition in European literature, their writings invariably insist that the colonizing power is absolutely representative of the city. Wordsworth's rustics have no place in Yeats's early oppositions between English materialism and Celtic closeness to nature and spirituality; nor do the peasants depicted by Manet and Monet qualify Senghor's view of the 'metropolitan' French culture.

While the form and content of nationalist literature often derive from a romanticized vision of the folk or pre-colonial culture (usually believed to be almost identical), most of the artists are also concerned with the problem of writing *for* the people, not merely *of* them. In a colonial situation the educated professional class has provided servants and clerks for the colonial administration, and its literature is addressed to readers in the 'mother' country. The writer who identifies with a nationalist movement seeks to break his ties with the exploiter and to identify with the exploited. He desires to speak for them and to them; he sees himself both as a teacher of the people and as being taught by them. The ambivalence which arises from the artist's dual perception of himself is revealed in Ron Karenga's essay prescribing norms for Afro-American artists, 'Black Cultural Nationalism' (1968). Quoting Senghor's claim that 'all African art has three characteristics: that is, it is functional, collective and committing or committed', Karenga, whose influence has been frequently acknowledged by Imamu Amiri Baraka (LeRoi Jones), goes on to define collective art as that which 'must be from the people and must be returned to the people in a form more colorful than it was in real life'. Karenga continues:

> To say that art must be collective, however, raises four questions. Number one, the question of popularization versus elevation; two, personality versus individuality; three, diversity in unity; and four, freedom *to* versus freedom *from*.
> The question of popularization versus elevation is an old one; what it really seeks to do is to ask and to answer the question whether or not art should be lowered to the level of the people or the people raised to the

level of art. Our contention is that if art is from the people, and for the people, there is no question of raising people to art or lowering art to the people, for they are one and the same thing.[13]

If art and the people are 'one and the same thing', what role does the artist play that a tape-recorder could not fulfil as well? And how does the poet then return the people to themselves 'in a form more colorful than . . . in real life'? Much as many Marxist critics have failed to come to grips with the conflicting prescriptions for socialist art – reflection of reality versus presentation of a socialist vision – Ron Karenga fails to deal satisfactorily with the question of popularization versus elevation. One finds the same evasion in dealing with the relationships between learning and teaching, speaking for or speaking to, in the essays and works of Yeats, Synge, and O'Casey, Senghor and Langston Hughes. But despite their emphasis on speaking for the people, Irish and African writers alike stress the role of the poet as teacher, prophet, and critic in their respective societies. Most have also been involved in trying to make their works readily available to the masses. Yeats, for instance, had his poems printed on broadsheets for cheap and easy distribution, projected a series of inexpensive editions of works by Irish writers, and saw the Abbey Theatre as the best means of reaching a public which seemed more receptive to the spoken than to the written word. The parallels with contemporary developments in the area of black American writing are close: witness the establishment of Broadside Press and the Third World Press, the increasing emphasis on guerilla theatre, the Spirit House founded by Baraka, and the stress on oral poetry.

Many of the Harlem Renaissance writers, on the other hand, were unconcerned about reaching the masses, addressing their works to a small upper-middle-class Negro and white elite, as Langston Hughes acknowledged in his autobiography, *The Big Sea*:

> But some Harlemites thought the millennium had come. They thought the Negro problem had been solved through art plus Gladys Bentley. They were sure the New Negro would lead a new life from then on in green pastures of tolerance created by Countee Cullen, Ethel Waters, Claude McKay, Duke Ellington, Bojangles and Alain Locke.
>
> I don't know what made any Negroes think that – except they were mostly intellectuals doing the thinking. The ordinary Negroes hadn't heard of the Negro Renaissance. And if they had, it hadn't raised their wages any.[14]

Langston Hughes raises one of the key issues faced by the artist concerned with a struggle for national independence: what relevance has his art to the active struggle for economic and political change? Can the writer be equally committed to art and political change? Must the committed artist subordinate his individual style and aesthetic judgment to the prescriptions of a political faction or ideology? In each of the movements discussed there has been a large group of intellectuals (and a larger group of non-intellectuals!) who have insisted that if people are going to sit around and write rather than get out on the streets and fight, then their work must meet certain ideological criteria in form and content. Thus Ron Karenga argues that all art can be judged on the social level and on the artistic level, and the social criteria are the most important. 'For all art that does not contribute to and support the Black Revolution is invalid, no matter how many lines and spaces are produced in proportion and symmetry and no matter how many sounds are boxed in and blown out and called music.'[15]

Karenga's views are similar to those of Fanon (whose *Wretched of the Earth* has been widely read by blacks in America). Fanon stresses the importance of cultural nationalism in the early stages of an independence struggle, for the work of the artist in recovering and celebrating a precolonial past helps to 'rehabilitate a nation and serve as the justification for the hope of a future national culture'.[16] Cultural nationalism corrects the distorted vision of the colonizer, who justified his presence by arguing that he brought history and culture to a people that had neither. 'In such a situation the claims of the native intellectual are not a luxury but a necessity in any coherent program.' But Fanon also insists that this concern with the pre-colonial heritage of the people should be merely a phase which must quickly give way to a concern with the present and with the political currents affecting the group. The writer should show the people how to react to contemporary economic and political events and issues, and he should realize that 'to fight for national culture means in the first place to fight for liberation of the nation, that material keystone which makes the building of a culture possible'.[17] Like Fanon, Padraic Pearse saw the work of the Gaelic League as a necessary stage: 'We had first to learn to know Ireland, to read the lineaments of her face, to understand the accents of her voice; to repossess ourselves, disinherited as we were, of her spirit and mind, re-enter into our mystical birthright. For this we went to school to the Gaelic League . . . But we do not propose to remain schoolboys forever.'[18] Only arms, Pearse maintained, could win Ireland's freedom; books must be replaced by guns, and ink by blood.

In Nigeria, writers like Achebe and Soyinka have also seen the recovery of the past and celebration of the nation's traditional culture as a necessary phase which must give way to other demands as the political situation changes. They have been even more critical than Fanon of the Negritude movement for its failure to meet those demands and for its creation of a 'black mystique', a criticism succinctly expressed in Soyinka's oft-quoted remark about tigritude. While the Nigerian writers agree with other nationalists about the importance of drawing upon traditional myths, legends, philosophies, and artistic techniques, they also insist on the necessity of examining the past critically and objectively, lest the mistakes of the past be repeated, or so that they can see, in Achebe's words, 'where the rain began to beat us'. Soyinka's *Dance of the Forests* suggests that the artist's role is to cut through the obfuscations caused by the Orator and the Court Historian, with their rhetoric about the glorious past, and to remain a detached critic of the inglorious reality – past and present.

For Soyinka and Achebe, the role of the artist is a continuing one in the struggle to liberate and build the new nation, not merely restricted to restoration of the past nor to the kind of guerilla theatre advocated by Fanon in his discussion of Keita Fodeiba's 'African Dawn', which he describes as 'a true invitation to thought, to demystification, and to battle', defining contemporary events and marking off 'the field in which were to be unfolded the actions and ideas around which the popular will would crystallize'.[19] Where many of the Nigerian writers, both in theory and practice, do agree with Fanon is that the artist should be concerned with 'demystification', whether it be of the world imposed by the colonizer or of the rhetoric and image propagated by those who took over when the colonizers appeared to leave. Obvious examples of works concerned with demystification include Okara's *The Voice*, Achebe's *Things Fall Apart* and *A Man of the People*, and Soyinka's *Kongi's Harvest*. These contemporary writers can be seen as continuing a role which poets assumed in many traditional African systems: particularly in West Africa the poet was often seen as the spokesman for public opinion and he alone was allowed to criticize, advise, and even abuse the king or chief of the clan with impunity.[20]

Whereas Fanon, Pearse, and Karenga see artistic efforts as a prelude to, and subordinate to, active involvement in a struggle for national independence, and whereas the Nigerian writers see the relationship between art and politics as a continuing dialectic, Senghor, like Yeats, has in ʾᵃᵗᵉ ˙ on the priority of art, with politics merely an aspect of the total culture.[21] He stated this position emphatically in an address to the First International Conference of Negro Writers and Artists in 1956, claiming that 'cultural liberation is an essential condition of political liberation', and that the Negro Renaissance would be the work of writers and artists rather than politicians: 'If white America concedes the claims of Negroes it will be because writers and artists, by showing the true visage of the race, have restored its dignity; if Europe is beginning to reckon with Africa, it is because her traditional sculpture, dancing, literature, and philosophy are henceforth forced upon an astonished world.'[22]

The question of the role of the artist in the moulding of the nation, the priority of aesthetic or political considerations, of survival of the spirit or physical survival, is dramatized again and again in Yeats's plays. The artist's duty to present noble images to influence the public is frequently stressed, not only by Yeats but also by other writers involved with the Abbey Theatre. Thus the preliminary manifesto advertising the New Irish Theatre reads in part:

> We will show that Ireland is not the home of buffoonery and easy senti-ment, as it has been represented, but the home of an ancient idealism. We are confident of the support of all Irish people, who are weary of misrepresentation, in carrying out a work that is outside all the political questions that divide us.[23]

The legendary figure of Cuchulain was to become one of the chief unifying images not only in Yeats's art but also for the Irish nationalists. Padraic Pearse is said to have invoked Cuchulain when the leaders of the Easter Rising took over the Dublin post office, where Cuchulain's statue now stands.

Yet the image of Cuchulain as individual warrior hero has little con-nection with the collective image of the Irish race which the younger Yeats, A. E., Katherine Tynan, Padraic Colum, and others promoted as typically Celtic – a people more inclined to commune with nature and the super-natural world than to plan and engage in successful military action. Similarly, the images of Chaka, or Toussaint L'Ouverture, or Nat Turner, or Malcolm X, all of whom appear again and again in the literature of decolonization as martyr-heroes, have little to do with the collective racial image promoted by Negritude, the Harlem Renaissance, and by some con-temporary black American writers, of a people distinguished by soul, feeling, and spirituality rather than hard-headed fighters and tacticians. A struggle between these sets of images suggested by LeRoi Jones's formula-tion, 'We are lovers and the sons of lovers, and warriors and the sons of warriors',[24] often takes place within plays and novels written in a national-istic context – the father-son conflicts in *Things Fall Apart*, *The Playboy of the Western World*, and Baldwin's *Blues for Mr Charlie*, for instance. Some-times the conflict is embodied in one character such as Walker Vessels in Jones's *The Slave*, or Ayamonn Breydon in O'Casey's *Red Roses for Me*, who is a poet and a labour leader, and a nationalist, encouraging his men to strike for 'a shilling in the shape of a new world'.

Contemporary black American writers generally share with the Irish dramatists the view that the poet's chief contribution to the nationalist cause lies in his role as creator and corrector of images. Addison Gayle echoes Shelley's comparison of art to a mirror which corrects distortions in the following exhortation to black writers:

> The revolutionary course leads through the destruction of the images, metaphors and symbols created by American mirror makers and forced upon Black people . . . Let our thinkers and creators of literature provide

us with images and symbols based upon the lives and exploits of such Afro-Americans [as Douglass, Garvey, Malcolm X, Harriet Tubman], let them show us images of ourselves in mirrors of our own construction.[25]

Although the works of those poets who belong to the Negritude movement include their share of image making and image correcting (namely, Damas's satires of the mulatto bourgeoisie, Césaire's *Tragedie du Roi Christophe* and *Saison au Congo*), their theory and practice have inclined to a view of poetry which is more akin to Nietzsche's than Aristotle's; that is, poetry is aligned with music rather than the visual arts; it invokes and evokes rather than represents. Both Senghor and Césaire have written of rhythm as the essential element in the creation of, and participation in, poetry, and both emphasize a concept of poetry as magic. The poet is a sorcerer whose incantations are a means of directing and realigning the life force. Thus the incantatory and ceremonial quality of Senghor's poems is their most distinctive quality.

Césaire's poetic practice shows a closer kinship to that of the French surrealists, however, than to Senghor's stately and sonorous lines, and like some of the surrealists he attempts to link the aims of Surrealism with those of Marxism. His poetic play, *Les Chiens se taisaient*, focuses on the relation between liberation, both political and psychological, and poetry, and embodies Césaire's definition of poetry as a 'possession and recreation of the world through the magic power of the word'.[26] In a letter to Lilyan Kesteloot, Césaire wrote: 'If I *name* with precision, . . . I believe that one restores to the object its personal value . . . its *value-power*. In naming flora and fauna in their strangeness, I add to their power; I partake of their power.'[27] This emphasis on the power of the word relates to the central concern of Act II of *Les Chiens* – the struggle for the power to define, for the master is the definer – and also to the word games played by the colonizers in Act I, where they protest that they did not *steal* the land from the people, but merely *captured* it. The political rebel who seeks to free his people must also be the poet who seeks through language to teach and to invoke and create a new world. The word is his last and most effective weapon:

> ma parole puissance de feu
> ma parole brisant la joue des tombes des cendres des
>   lanternes
> ma parole qu'aucune chimie ne saurait apprivoiser
> ni ceindre.[28]

The concept of poetry as magic and of words as weapons is also found frequently in the poetry of contemporary Afro-American writers, many of whom have been directly or indirectly influenced by the Negritude writers and by such works as *Muntu* by Jahnheinz Jahn. Imamu Amiri Baraka's 1969 volume of poetry was entitled *Black Magic*, and his 'Black Art' has become a manifesto for the movement of that name:

> . . . We want 'poems that kill'.
> Assassin poems, Poems that shoot
> guns, Poems that wrestle cops into alleys
> and take their weapons leaving them dead
> with tongues pulled out and sent to Ireland . . .
>
> Poems scream poison gas on beasts in green berets
> Clean out the world for virtue and love,
> Let there be no love poems written
> until love can exist freely and
> cleanly. Let Black People understand
> that they are the lovers and the sons
> of lovers and warriors and sons
> of warriors Are poems & poets &
> all the loveliness here in the world
>
> We want a black poem. And a
> Black World.
> Let the world be a Black Poem
> And let all Black People Speak This Poem
> Silently
> or LOUD

Though the violence of its style and imagery is alien to the Irish or Harlem Renaissance, or generally to the work of the Nigerian writers, Baraka's poem does articulate much that is typical of nationalist literature. It affirms the power of poetry and attempts to reconcile 'lovers and warriors', yet the very determination to eliminate the gap between words and concrete action suggests the questioning of the efficacy of those words. Baraka also brings together in this poem the role of the poet as teacher, prophet, and leader who awakens and inspires the people, and the vision of the people as themselves 'poems & poets &/all the loveliness here in the world'. And, finally, Baraka's poem embodies the two directions in which nationalist literature and theory tend – on the one hand emphasizing an Aristotelian concept of art as the mirroring of images from which people may learn, on the other aligning poetry with invocation, with magic, with rhythm and sound, and seeking to eliminate the gap between words and things.

NOTES

1. James Weldon Johnson, *The Book of American Negro Poetry*, New York, Harcourt, Brace & Co., 1931, p. 41.
2. *The New Negro*, New York, Atheneum, 1968, p. 7.
3. See especially *The Negro in American Fiction*, New York, 1937.
4. At a conference hosted by Central Washington State College, Ellensburg, Washington, Spring 1967. Stokely Carmichael also participated.
5. Quoted by L. P. Curtis, *Anglo–Saxons and Celts*, Bridgeport, Conn., University of Bridgeport Press, 1968, p. 84.
6. *On the Study of Celtic Literature*, New York, Macmillan, 1904, pp. 76–8.
7. Frantz Fanon, *The Wretched of the Earth*, trans. C. Farrington, New York, Grove Press, p. 43.
8. Trans. C. L. Markmann, New York, Grove Press, 1967, p. 18.
9. 'Sur l'exoticisme colonial', *La nouvelle critique*, May 1959, p. 139 (my translation).
10. *The Book of American Negro Poetry*, p. 4.
11. *Black Orpheus*, trans. Samuel Allen, *Présence Africaine*, 1956, pp. 50–1.
12. 'On the De-Anglicization of Ireland', a speech delivered in 1891 and reprinted in *1,000 Years of Irish Prose*, V. Mercier and D. Greene (eds), New York, Grosset & Dunlop, 1961, p. 81.
13. *The Black Aesthetic*, ed. Addison Gayle, New York, Doubleday: Anchor, 1972, p. 34.
14. op. cit., New York, Hill & Wang, 1963, p. 228.
15. *The Black Aesthetic*, p. 31.
16. op. cit., p. 210.
17. ibid., p. 211.
18. 'The Coming Revolution', in V. Mercier and D. Greene (eds.) op. cit., p. 235
19. *The Wretched of the Earth*, p. 227.
20. Ruth Finnegan, *Oral Literature in Africa*, Oxford, Clarendon Press, 1970, p. 120.
21. Lilyan Kesteloot, *Les Écrivains noirs de langue français*, Brussels, University of Brussels Press, 1965, p. 92.
22. 'The Spirit of Civilization', *Présence Africaine* (special issue, 1956: English edition), p. 51.
23. W. B. Yeats, *Autobiography*, New York, Macmillan, 1953, p. 132.
24. See 'Black Art', quoted below.
25. 'The Politics of Revolution', *Black World*, June 1972, pp. 10–11.
26. G. R. Coulthard, 'The French West Indian Background of Negritude', *Caribbean Quarterly*, VIII, 3, December 1961, p. 130.
27. Lilyan Kesteloot (ed.), *Aimé Césaire*, Paris, Seghers, 1962, p. 197 (my translation).
28. *Les Chiens*, *Présence Africaine*, 1956, p. 46.

Iconoclasts Both: Wole Soyinka and LeRoi Jones

Chikwenye Okonjo Ogunyemi

By the 1960s, the role of blacks as pariah in the world was ending as they declared their manhood: many West African countries had gained independence; East and Central Africa were in ferment; the black Americans had taken to the streets protesting against their second-class citizenship. The riotous spirit was reflected in a disturbing manner in black literary works. In a virile voice black writers protested against indifferent Establishments, black or white. They were angry and in their idealism were understandably in a hurry to battle with and change the world to make it better for blacks. Thus the African voice, the black voice, strident, raised against years of mental, physical, and economic subjugation under whites and traditional usage, declared its coming of age while underscoring the problems that are attendant on such independence. Wole Soyinka and LeRoi Jones were two of those black voices.

Wole Soyinka, a Nigerian, and LeRoi Jones, a black American, were born in 1934. Each married first a white then a black woman. In their literary careers, they have expressed their ideas in different genres: the essay, the novel, poetry, and most pertinent to us, drama. In politics, they are revolutionaries, determined to break the status quo by any power legitimately at their disposal. Their iconoclastic tendencies are sometimes reflected in their works.

It will be of interest to look into the works of these two black writers with disparate backgrounds whose biographical sketches appear to be similar. How do the African and the black American cope with the crises of modern existence? For a tentative answer we can examine two plays they published in 1964 when each was 30 – Soyinka's *The Strong Breed* and LeRoi Jones's *Dutchman*.

In both plays we see the democratizing quality, the anonymity in part of the characterization, the use of art for a definite purpose, the element of protest and iconoclasm that seem to be the distinguishing features of black or African art. Thomas Hodgkin's conception of African art puts in a nutshell the spirit that informs the works and ideas of the two playwrights:

> African art is essentially a collective art, done for everyone with the participation of everyone. It is a practical art . . . It is a committed art: the artist mirrors his people, his time, his history, but he mirrors them from a definite personal point of view. And it is an art which virtually goes on all the time.[1]

Soyinka and LeRoi Jones portray their heroes interacting with others in this African manner, their way of coping with the torment that is part of modern living. Occasionally their portrayal is anti-stereotypic. They also modify European myths to suit their own purposes, ending with a type of art that is unique to blacks.

For the purposes of this article, I shall restrict my discussion of the two playwrights to their plays *The Strong Breed* and *Dutchman*. The two plays will be viewed in relation to each other to cast some light on areas of similarity engendered by cross-influences and the black collective unconscious; it is significant that these two writers with differing backgrounds produced two similar plays contemporaneously. The points to be investigated are the theme of the outsider in conjunction with the handling of some stereotypes; the mythical background and the scapegoat mechanism employed; the roles of mobs and women in the two works; and, briefly, the technique used in both plays. The iconoclastic tendencies in the works will be pinpointed.

Commenting on Soyinka's attitude towards life generally, Oyin Ogunba asserts that 'Soyinka has the reputation in certain circles in Nigeria . . . of being the artist *par excellence* in an ultra-modern, twentieth century sense, a man against the Establishment, a firm believer in the absolute freedom of the individual'.[2] This attitude is demonstrated in *The Strong Breed* in his portrayal of Eman, the archetypal outsider and protector of the underdog. LeRoi Jones, on the other hand, with different preoccupations and a slightly different battle to fight against the Establishment, was to insist on 'Unity against individualism and division; *Self Determination* against domination by others in whatever we propose';[3] these are his ideals for a new revolution, one that is not dissimilar to Soyinka's struggle.

In the two plays under consideration both playwrights make serious criticisms of their societies, their closely-knit tendencies, their exclusiveness that makes outsiders of those who are strangers or those who are different in any way. Their criticism is rather unsettling. Consequently, both produce black art which LeRoi Jones has described as revolutionary art; that is, revolutionary art by black artists.[4] Eldred Jones's comment on Soyinka, that 'If the individual will is so important, society must enable it to be exercised freely',[5] can be applied to the freedom that the black will demands. The idea is to break the confining chain which limits the liberty of the black man, aesthetic or otherwise. They therefore explore that seemingly enduring African spirit which enables the black man to cope with a distressing way of life, an enduring spirit which his opponent has misinterpreted and taken advantage of. The status quo receives the brunt of their attacks in their ultimate goal for total black emancipation. For Soyinka, this means emancipation from the traditional customs and religions that could have debilitating effects on the black man; for LeRoi Jones it means the establishment of a separate black identity, distinguishable from that of the other Americans.[6]

In handling this situation, the theme of the outsider is important. Where LeRoi Jones treats whites as enemies of blacks, Soyinka portrays the black man as his own enemy, making an outsider of his potential saviour.

The outsider in *The Strong Breed* is Eman; he is a stranger not just because he comes from a village different from that in which he resides, he is also an outsider because he is literate in a village of illiterates, a difference that could engender some conflict from a philosophical viewpoint. The man who is not a 'son of the soil', in Nigerian parlance, is automatically treated as a second-class citizen with the consequent humiliations. Indeed, resorting to cruelty against the outsider is a protective reaction by the insiders since they view the outsider with trepidation, looking on him as an iconoclast determined to destroy the basis of their society. Eman fits the role of the outsider also when he makes a 'harlot' of Sunma, a relationship that Jaguna, her father, views with disdain. Furthermore, Eman is a teacher, one set apart to bring light to ignorant minds. This makes him an antagonist to the whole village because a teacher effects change, a circumstance that would be resented in a conservative society. He is also a clinician, a healer of the body; he will later be called upon to heal the mind, by making the final sacrifice as a carrier of their sins.

Stressing the idea of being a stranger, Eman warns Sunma: 'Let me continue a stranger – especially to you. Those who have much to give fulfil themselves only in total loneliness.'[7] Here, Eman states categorically his growing awareness of his calling as a saviour. He will remain alone and estranged to the very end, for which he will pay the ultimate penalty by acting as carrier for the village, a role assigned to strangers.

Eman is not the only outsider in the play. Ifada, in a way his *alter ego*, is another stranger set apart because of his idiocy. Eman (like Ifada) was not willing to be a carrier initially. Ifada is the unwilling part of him, unwilling to become a carrier as Eman had been in his own village where he belonged to a line of carriers, the strong breed. Both run away in terror when the brutality of being a carrier becomes clear. Ifada is also Eman's conscience, that inner voice that tells him he can no longer run away from his responsibility. So, Ifada plays a crucial role in making Eman face reality as Lula in *Dutchman* was to make Clay stop hiding under the cloak of Uncle Tomism. The Eman-Ifada psychological situation is reminiscent of the Captain-Leggatt relationship in Conrad's 'The Secret Sharer'. Eman and the Captain risk all to protect the other self. As outsiders, Eman and Ifada are ideal as carriers in this village that uses strangers as sacrificial lambs to rid itself of its curses and sins. Ifada acts as carrier temporarily, but, terrified by the brutality, he runs to Eman for refuge. Both Eman and Ifada are part of a continuum, carriers as of right in both villages. The strong breed in one village can thus be equated with the idiot/stranger in the other since they are only useful to both communities as carriers. It is therefore not far-fetched to say that Ifada is the child and the idiotic part of Eman, qualities which prevent Eman from heeding Sunma's pleadings, making him offer, in a romantic moment, to replace Ifada as carrier without knowing the full implications of such an offer. When Eman is taken away and Ifada returns, the latter becomes miraculously changed, developing into a source of strength to the much weakened Sunma. To all intents and purposes, he has now replaced Eman. Indeed, at the end of the play, Soyinka directs: 'Ifada hugs the effigy [Eman symbolically] to him, stands above Sunma' (p. 145). Thus the relationship of Eman and Ifada is a see-saw type of relationship, each of immense import to the other. Eman's problem had partly been one of identity – not knowing who he is, that is, his destiny as a carrier. His initial escape from his village was therefore fruitless. Ifada's fear-stricken eyes open the world of the inevitable, the world of the carrier for Eman, making him finally volunteer for the sacrifice.

Sunma is the third outsider in the play. Replying to Eman's statement, 'Sometimes you talk as if you were a stranger too' (p. 120), she declares: 'I wonder if I really sprang from here. I know they are evil and I am not. From the oldest to the smallest child, they are nourished in evil and unwholesomeness in which I have no part' (p. 121). As an outsider/insider, she perceives the ambience of evil surrounding her village. As penalty for being a stranger she is, but for Ifada, alone at the end of the play, a wreck of her former self, broken by the trauma of fruitlessly trying to protect a loved one. The old year has taken quite a toll.

From Soyinka's depiction we can see that the iconoclastic tendencies and the stereotype work on two levels – in the play and outside it. In the play, Eman shakes the traditional basis of the people's religion by offering to be a carrier, an unprecedented event. As we shall see later, his role as a carrier and his mode of carrying out his duties transform the lives of the people; their belief in their religion has been disoriented. Eman bequeaths to them a new religion and a new way of life. Outside the play, Soyinka makes a swipe at the romantic conception of the primitive and innocent African rural society waiting anxiously for the civilizing influences of Christianity. He presents us instead with an evil and complex society, trying to achieve its mundane aspirations. Meanwhile it helplessly resists the incursion of foreign religion and ideas.

In LeRoi Jones's *Dutchman* the theme of the outsider has racial reverberations. The typical American outsider is the black educated man, difficult to place in the social ladder. He is doubly an outsider as he no longer belongs to the blacks, separated as he is in his aspirations and because of the potpourri nature of his culture, a factor that is reflected in the mythical and historical background of the play. *Vis-à-vis* the whites, he is considered an Uncle Tom, meek, aping white ways, and so desirous of their women. LeRoi Jones initially presents this Uncle Tom stereotype in his portrayal of Clay, only to blast it in his exploration of the hidden aspect of the Uncle Tom – the revolutionary aspect. Thus, Lula and the American society which she represents experience a psychologically unbalancing phenomenon in LeRoi Jones's presentation of the erstwhile easy-going Uncle Tom. His Uncle Tom is an iceberg whose destructive potentialities are so well hidden that they take their victim by surprise. Lula the liberal thinks she knows Clay; but his tirade is unexpected, arousing primitive instincts for self-protection in her. For Lula and the society to maintain their equilibrium, society must connive at getting rid of the outsider, as we see in Clay's instance. His character is not individualized, emphasizing the democratizing quality of black art. Clay is the chosen black representative, and his role, with its suffering and pain, is for the benefit of all black men. Indeed, one can envisage a black audience reacting to his tirade with punctuations of 'say it, brother', 'right on', 'soul brother', etc., as he puts into words what had been in black minds. He is a typical black, educated middle-class man, one of many on the journey through American history. The antagonist is Lula, whose confrontation with Clay represents that great, unconsummated stereotypic romance between the white woman and the black American man. Receiving an inkling of the unseen reaches of this outsider, she unleashes her violence in typical frontier fashion, for these are the frontiers of the black-white relation, with its ignorance, its pretensions, its sexuality, its deceptiveness, its violence and blood bath.

Lula seems to have won this round but it is only seemingly so. Clay, however, has lived fully in his moment of outburst and, like Hemingway's Francis Macomber, he is a hero who has enjoyed a triumph though it is short-lived. Lula's murderous career indicates what she is – a mad criminal – as she waits to tackle her next victim. Her violence against Clay or all black men is a representation, from LeRoi Jones's point of view, of the emasculating nature of the relationship between white women and black men. Her use of a knife demonstrates symbolically black penis envy; it adequately illustrates the psychological and sexual undertones in the relationship. The disturbing nature of LeRoi Jones's portrayal is consequently obvious as he dismisses one popularly held opinion after the other.

Thus Wole Soyinka and LeRoi Jones explore the theme of the outsider, stressing the trauma that is associated with the unknown in any society and the obsession to rid society of such iconoclasts. The stereotypes that are believed in demonstrate how far from the truth is man's knowledge of the outsider. In their portrayal, there is an underlying criticism of the hostility of man for the unknown, for the outsider, to the extent that to maintain societal balance man is prepared to commit murder to rid himself of the outsider. The will for survival is sometimes predatory.

Traditionally, the outsider has had to play the role of the scapegoat, most of the time unwillingly. These two playwrights present the scapegoat as a saviour, a type of Christ, who carries away the sins of the world in order, ostensibly, to make the world a better place.

Soyinka's Eman with his calling as a teacher and clinician is a type of Christ.[8] He had recognized his role early when he told Omae, 'A man must go on his own, go where no one can help him, and test his strength' (pp. 138–9). Before Eman emerges as a Christ figure, he and his lover Omae are initially cast in the Adam and Eve archetype. In this regard one considers their innocence. Moreover, the tutor is at once God and the snake. The tutor as God cynically asks if Omae had come to steal from his fruit trees (Eman?). The sexual undertones in this scene are inescapable, emphasized as they are by Omae's occasional bashfulness. Is Eman's training for manhood just for circumcision? Is it a painful ordeal? Furthermore, we see the tutor as snake lecherously advancing towards Omae, pinpointing the animality of carnal knowledge. All these remind us of Adam and Eve, an idea that is again stressed in the tutor's statement: 'Eman had broken a strong taboo' (p. 139). Like Adam and Eve, Eman and Omae are banished from the seemingly idyllic existence in the paradise/village and are thrown to the vagaries of the world. However, Eman moves from adolescence to achieve that manhood he had been training for by taking a stand against the snake/tutor. Adam and Eve are revolutionaries.

30

Eman starts as Adam and later metamorphoses to that vital part of the line of Adam – Jesus Christ, who in turn is a revolutionary. As an iconoclast, Eman breaks a taboo, leaves the village, resents Omae's death which was predictable, refuses to take up a career as a carrier (here, he has meta-morphosed into Christ who abandoned the trade of carpenter for a higher calling), and goes to another village, where he answers the call of his blood by finally becoming a carrier. His iconoclastic tendencies continue in Sunma's village where he spoils their purification ceremony by escaping before the ritual has been completed so that the efficacy of the ritual is doubtful. Whatever happens, the village will never be the same again after his life and death there. That disruptive element associated with Christ is immanent in Eman's life in these villages. In his presentation, Soyinka superimposes African religion on Christian mythology, each vying for supremacy in a rather disconcerting manner. At the end we realize that a new way of life has been born, the old and the new religions co-existing in doubtful harmony as is the case in modern Nigeria.

Throughout all these events, the enigmatic father of Eman, mortal, yet seemingly immortal, all-powerful, a spiritual guide, evoked at a moment of crisis, like God with Christ, cannot or will not change the course of events. His presence as a spirit, as well as Omae's during Eman's crisis, underscore that African factor which Senghor hints at of man's intimate relationship with his ancestors and spirits, particularly at a time of spiritual distress.[9] In a way, Eman's evocation of the past is the traditional worship of one's ancestors, a process that is psychologically reassuring for him.

The sick girl's role in the play is noteworthy. Wilfred Cartey sees her as 'a miniature of the village' with its evil propensities looking for a carrier to make it healthy.[10] Ogunba sees the girl and her effigy partly as comic relief.[11] To me, her actions seem to be marked with high seriousness. When she puts Eman's clothes on the effigy, the effigy becomes an iconographic representation of Eman. The battering of the effigy, its eventual crucifixion in the belief that it will take away sickness with the old year, presage the role that Eman will play. Sunma realizes this instinctively, hence her agita-tion, for the girl has a mimetic resemblance to Jaguna.

However, one has to ask how efficacious the whole ritual of the carrier is. In taking Eman as carrier, according to his father's predictions, the village has committed the heinous sin of thievery, an act which compounds the attempt to free themselves of sin.

The two villages are the world in microcosm, with its attendant evil. In Eman's village we see signs of sexuality, the curse on Omae-Eve and the other women who have to die on giving birth to the strong breed, the need for redemption with the carrier as the central figure in the village. In Sunma's village evil is so rife that they habitually groom an ignorant stranger or idiot to carry out their unpleasant duties for them. With this depiction, Soyinka, as I have observed, wipes out the idea of a romantic, idyllic, rural life in the African village. Evil is as all-pervasive here as it is in the rest of the world; violence exists. The seeming fruitlessness of the cleansing exercise is further compounded in the sin of murder – the killing of an outsider, a hated person. It becomes a vicious cycle as the Sisyphean duty of the carrier is effected year after year.

But Soyinka's stand is ambivalent with his depiction of a miraculously changed Ifada. Eman's role as carrier and his death have effected a visible improvement in Ifada's physique, making a man of the erstwhile idiotic, drooling child. This is in keeping with the tradition of the enigmatic Ogun, the Yoruba god linked with death and renewal at the same time. The speechlessness, awe, and wonder of the crowd is relevant in this context. With his death, Eman ushers in a new year, a period for adjustment, a time for change which Oroge and the sceptical Jaguna recognize in spite of themselves. The whole scapegoat mechanism, with the idea of the saviour, is couched in ambiguity in *The Strong Breed*, the ambiguity which has become part of the culture of modern Africa. The spirit that informs the play is distressingly real.

Like Eman, Clay in his role as a would-be poet is a mentor – a Baudelaire changing not just the course of poetry but also the course of the poetry of black life. We have an indication of the black struggle to escape from mental and aesthetic domination in order to assert a unique black identity as Baudelaire's poetry was distinctive.

Apart from being a fighter for the freedom of the mind, Clay is also conceived as a latter-day Adam with Lula/Eve tempting him with the offer of an apple. As with Soyinka's hero, Clay too metamorphoses into the archetype of Christ – Lula refers to him as 'My Christ, My Christ'; Lula needs Clay's blood for redemption, redemption from her sins as Eve and as a psychological lyncher – her verbal attack launched against Clay at the beginning of their meeting is a psychological lynching, with its arbitrariness, its abruptness, and its injustice. She will also need his blood as Christ to cleanse her of the greater sin of physical lynching when she stabs him fatally in her insanity. With the portrayal of Lula, LeRoi Jones gives us an anti-stereotype of the good liberal that the black man had been persistently fed on. Disturbing and pessimistic though he may seem, he presents us with what he feels is the truth in the black-liberal relationship. As a poet, Clay is a visionary. His encounter with Lula brings him down to earth, for in his role as an Uncle Tom he was running away from his true revolutionary self as Eman was running away from his duty as a carrier.

Just as *The Strong Breed* dealt with Eman's manhood, *Dutchman* is about Clay's manhood, the black man's manhood. And just as Soyinka regards drama as 'a revolutionary art form',[12] so LeRoi Jones insists that black theatre 'should also be an act of liberation';[13] for Clay, the play shows his liberation from the three-piece suit and the domination by white cultural aspirations. As he is liberated from Uncle Tomism the black audience becomes vicariously liberated too. In its conscious didacticism, Clay's final outburst is revolutionary, reversing roles to show the white man 'his place', and to tell the black man what to do.

The two plays are thus rituals in a sense. They both involve the reader or audience in a participatory role producing an emotional cleansing following the blood bath; after the experience life can no longer really be the same. They open a new year for us, a new way of comprehension of life, and a fresh approach to battling with its vicissitudes. The utilitarian quality is what distinguishes modern black art from modern Western art. LeRoi Jones arouses emotion on a political and social issue since Lula is not the only murderer in that train. Clay's murder is done collectively with the people helping Lula to get rid of all circumstantial evidence. With the cyclical ending we realize that there are more Clays and communal guilt is all-pervading. LeRoi Jones's play is a criticism against collective sin that would need unceasing atonement, a factor that one also has to reckon with in Soyinka's play. One's solace as far as Eman and Clay are concerned is Claude McKay's sentiment in his sonnet, 'If We Must Die':

> If we must die, O let us nobly die,
> So that our precious blood may not be shed
> In vain; then even the monsters we defy
> Shall be constrained to honor us though dead! ...
>
> Like men we'll face the murderous, cowardly pack,
> Pressed to the wall, dying, but fighting back!

Such is the emotion that these two plays arouse.

The roles of the anonymous mobs in both plays have many points of similarity. Their passivity in the face of brutality and their indifference to the fate of someone who is their hero are a criticism against black unreceptiveness towards their leaders.

The mob in *The Strong Breed*, like that associated with Jesus Christ's demise, has experienced something awesome and inexpressible. Jaguna tries to describe their reaction when he says: 'One and all they looked up at the man and words died in their throats.' Oroge declares quite succinctly: 'It was no common sight.' Then Jaguna: 'One by one they crept off like sick dogs. Not one could raise a curse' (p. 146). Something indescribable has been added to their experience. In a way, the carrier has succeeded in making a new life for the benefit of these anonymous people. Jaguna might not experience change, but every other character knew, like the three magi, that they had experienced something and there was no more clinging to the old gods. This play therefore demonstrates the groping for a new way of life, the discarding of old gods who demanded blood for a new one whose desires are yet enigmatic.

The collectivity that we see in African art we also experience with *Dutchman* and the role of the mob. Lula intuitively knew she had the support of the crowd so she could go on with her criminal act, first emasculating Clay, then knifing him. But her crime could be a catalyst arousing black men to action in self-defence. The acquiescence of the mob demonstrates the connivance of both black and white people to the racism perpetrated on black people. Clay is slain for having arrived at manhood with his courage to say 'no' to Lula. For a hitherto docile people, the 'no' is revealing, disconcerting, and unprecedented, triggering off a psychological imbalance in the black-white relationship: LeRoi Jones's fresh approach to racism is epochal and must have contributed to the psychological boost black Americans had in the sixties. It is significant that a performance of *Dutchman* was cancelled for fear it would whip up feelings and cause a riot following the death of Martin Luther King, Jr.[14]

The role of women in the plays is crucial to the understanding of the heroes in both works. Eman in *The Strong Breed* is imperceptive, a point that is symbolized by the all-pervading darkness throughout the play. To the very end, as he falls into the trap set for him under the sacred trees by the stream where he needs must quench his thirst, we realize he has kept himself in the dark too long. This blundering hero reaches his decisions through the timely intervention of women. Unknown to him, while he was under his tutor he was in the ambience of sin. Omae reveals the truth of the situation to him. Then he begins his career as a Wandering Jew (a legend that is also evoked in *Dutchman*), seeking the meaning of life and shirking his responsibility both as a father and the carrier-designate in his village. The play opens at a time for decisive action in his life – he does not know that he has reached the peak of his unwelcome career as a carrier. Sunma, more far-seeing, uses her female intuition to attempt to prevent him from the final sacrifice. His ignorance is inexcusable but the inevitability of his destiny makes him reject Sunma's escapist plan. Moreover, Ifada's eyes tell him he has come to the end of the road, so he goes forward courageously and willingly (for he is not coerced) to be carrier. In a way he has won a moral victory over the traditionalists, Jaguna and Oroge, by going to them voluntarily, contrary to normal practice. Furthermore, he did not know that Omae would die, although his father knew, nor did he completely apprehend that he had to be a carrier because of the nature of the tradition in his family. His more discerning father saw these things. He did not know that he could not study for his manhood under the tutor's direction but had to go out to the world under difficult circumstances in order to establish his manhood. He also did not know the implications of being a carrier in Sunma's village. The lack of vital knowledge on the part of Eman is a shortcoming that eventually leads him to his doom. It emphasizes his separateness, his aloneness, his existence in an ivory tower away from the people he was meant to serve. This sin he will have to pay for with his life. Throughout all the darkness, Sunma brings light (physically too) and enlightens Eman about his precarious position.

Clay's case is equally agonizing. His ignorance, like Eman's, is symbolized by the darkness of the 'earth's belly', the subway, with its dim lights flashing by rapidly. At the stops, light is occasionally cast on the train as it moves relentlessly on in its journey. That light is the moment of truth, inescapable and inexorable. Clay's darkness is phenomenal: he does not know who he is; he does not know that his conversation with Lula is not just about sexuality but about his life and his manhood. Lula clarifies the situation for him. Like Eman, once guided, he gropingly arrives at his identity as a black, and as a man, before his death. The question of identity is highlighted by Clay's outburst: 'If I'm a middle-class fake white man . . . let me be. And let me be in the way I want' (*Dutchman*, p. 229).[15] The key-word there is *if*; he does not know who he is.

When the heroes finally discover their true selves their female counter-parts are in for a great shock. As the heroes move towards their true identity the women, Sunma and Lula, lose their sanity and their hold over them so that at the end the heroes emerge independent, able to follow their instincts. These saviours have had a chance, like Christ, of giving up their lives for their cause. They have lived fully and that is their victory. The world they leave behind is a different world. Like King Lear, their limited vision could have affected their effectiveness as purgative agents. But the tragedy of the futility of life is not their own fate; as they die they leave something positive behind – a new way of life for their people. Their sacrifices were therefore invaluable. Indeed, the Lula who will take on the next black victim is in a state of shock and she is not like the Lula at the beginning of the play. Too much has happened to damage her liberal ego. She will no longer have the self-confidence of 'knowing' the next Uncle Tom. She might become an aggressor turned victim because her tactics with the next black man must needs be different and this might be her undoing. A change in black-white relationship has occurred in spite of the ending which, on a superficial interpretation, appears pessimistic.

What Soyinka and LeRoi Jones have succeeded in putting across is the necessity for complementarity between black men and black women, for the common good in Soyinka's instance, and in LeRoi Jones's, the need for caution and in-depth thinking on the part of the black man when he is confronted by a white woman. As for the individual who is part of the mob, the writers underscore the fact that he has an active role to play; non-action is criminal. All this is shamelessly didactic – it is art not merely for pleasure but art to awaken a slumbering, maltreated people, unaware of their potentialities.

Alain Ricard has pointed out that the cinematographic effect is vital to the presentation of the flashbacks or time past in *The Strong Breed*.[16] The use of the flashback by Soyinka could be confusing to the audience (not to the armchair reader) used to a mental rather than a physical evocation of the past on the stage. The situation is necessitated by an African need, for as Eman approaches his death, in true African belief, the spirits of dead relatives and friends come to meet him to welcome him to the new life in store for him. It is a happy conclusion of ancestral worship, being at one with the dear departed at a time of terror preceding death. The two worlds, the living and the dead (or the past) merge, a process that is credible to the African with his mystical propensities. This can of course be explained away psychologically in the sense that Eman wills the presence of his loved ones in his dire need.

The use of cinematographic techniques is also a prerequisite in the production of *Dutchman*. The clever use of light is necessary to give the idea of motion; the contrasting use of light and darkness will help to create a symbolic atmosphere emphasizing the darkness and confused state of black minds (and white) with the occasional glimmer of perception.

The fact that both playwrights do not want a break in the course of the action is in itself cinematographic although the brevity of the one-act plays also makes a break unnecessary. The fast pace helps to build up emotion right to the point of the death of the hero, keeping the reader or audience keyed up emotionally to the end. The cacophonous sounds of the train in *Dutchman* and of the lorry and people in the chase in *The Strong Breed* provide the 'musical' background which reaches a crescendo as the death of the hero occurs; then the noise peters out. The sounds help to create the disturbing atmosphere of the plays just as much as the iconoclastic viewpoints expressed are equally disturbing. Mood therefore matches thought.

LeRoi Jones, later known as Imamu Amiri Baraka (Imamu means 'spiritual leader'), had, in 1964, already envisaged himself as a spiritual leader, an idea embedded in his conception of Clay. It is now commonly accepted that Clay is identical to the young, racially uninvolved LeRoi Jones. LeRoi Jones's feeling of being an outsider[17] is highlighted in the unfulfilled life of Clay. Wole Soyinka's romantic affair, battling against the Nigerian government, his spiritual leadership in both artistic ideas and political thought, show him to be of the same calibre as LeRoi Jones. That Eman in his romantic role is Soyinka himself is not farfetched. What is striking about them is the fact that these two black writers, with seemingly dissimilar backgrounds, were able, at the time they were 30, and in the same year, to produce two very similar works. That the African heritage, indelible as it is, yet sometimes unidentifiable, has been the guiding spirit of the two black writers there can be little doubt. The African heritage speaks for itself; it permits them to take a foreign myth or a foreign idea and combine it with what is essentially African to create a new type of art. Thus the plays by their very nature bring across to the audience different facts about modern black life, its multifarious culture, and its hopes for survival.

In the final analysis, what the playwrights have achieved is twofold; they present us with characters who are iconoclasts, unsettling the people they have to interact with in the plays; outside the context of the plays, the playwrights, as iconoclasts, use the drama as a medium to unsettle their audiences in presenting us with characters and ideas that are far removed from our expectations. This psychological disorientation, inside and outside the works, is their distinguishing contribution to the new black art.

NOTES

1. Thomas L. Hodgkin, 'The African Renaissance', in *African Heritage: Intimate Views of the Black Africans from Life, Lore and Literature*, ed. Jacob Drachler, New York, The Crowell-Collier Press, 1963, p. 278.
2. Oyin Ogunba, *The Movement of Transition: A Study of the Plays of Wole Soyinka*, Ibadan, Ibadan University Press, 1975, p. 6.
3. Imamu Amiri Baraka (né LeRoi Jones), 'Black "Revolutionary" Poets Should Also Be Playwrights', *Black World*, XXI, 6, April 1972, p. 6.
4. ibid., p. 4.
5. Eldred Durosimi Jones, *The Writing of Wole Soyinka*, London, Heinemann, 1973, p. 12.
6. Baraka, op. cit., p. 6.
7. Wole Soyinka, *The Strong Breed*, in *Wole Soyinka: Collected Plays 1*,

London, Oxford University Press, 1973, p. 125. All subsequent references are to this edition and appear in the text.

8. Jones, op. cit., p. 49.
9. See Hodgkin, op. cit., p. 278.
10. Wilfred Cartey, *Whispers from a Continent: The Literature of Contemporary Black Africa*, London, Heinemann, 1971, p. 338.
11. Ogunba, op. cit., p. 118.
12. Wole Soyinka, 'Drama and the Revolutionary Ideal' and three interviews, *In Person Achebe, Awoonor, and Soyinka*, ed. Karen L. Morell, Washington, 1975, pp. 59–130. Also, see *African Writers Talking*, ed. Dennis Duerden and Cosmo Pieterse, London, Heinemann, 1972, p. 170.
13. Michael Coleman, 'What is Black Theater? An Interview with Imamu Amiri Baraka', *Black World*, 20, 1971, p. 32.
14. Daphne S. Reed, 'LeRoi Jones: High Priest of the Black Arts Movement', *Educational Theatre Journal*, XXI, 1, March 1970, p. 58.
15. Clinton F. Oliver, Introduction to LeRoi Jones's *Dutchman*, in *Contemporary Black Drama: From a Raisin in the Sun to No Place to Be Somebody*, ed. Clinton F. Oliver and Stephanie Sills, New York, Charles Scribner's Sons, 1971, p. 211. All subsequent references are to this edition and appear in the text.
16. Alain Ricard, 'Théâtre et nationalisme: Wole Soyinka et LeRoi Jones', *Présence Africaine*, 1972, p. 104.
17. Oliver and Sills, op. cit., p. 209

The American Background in *Why Are We So Blest?*[1]

Robert Fraser

The interplay between Africa and the Americas has left us not only an historical, but also a plentiful literary legacy. Since the horror of forced migration and the slave trade ceased at the beginning of the last century, a growing flow of visitors, first a trickle and now a steady stream, have crossed or recrossed the Atlantic in both directions seeking various sorts of experience. American writers such as Hemingway, Bellow, and Theroux have borne witness.[2] On their side, African writers have not been slow to state, sometimes trenchantly, the impact which the New World has made on them. From Senghor's *New York*[3] to John Pepper Clark's *America, Their America*,[4] the views expressed have often been controversial in tone. Increasingly these visitors have been students, more recently on the trail of some sort of postgraduate study; for – and it is a point to watch – beginning with Doctors Aggrey and Azikwe, the decision to study in the States rather than in Europe has often been as much a political as an academic one. It has been one way of avoiding the colonizing grasp of either Britain or France. We should not, therefore, be surprised if America often finds itself confronted by scholars of markedly radical awareness, or if the perspective on American life encountered in the books they may come to write should be shaped by a polemical vision. These remarks prove illuminating when we come to consider the work of the Ghanaian novelist Ayi Kwei Armah.

Armah's third published novel *Why Are We So Blest?* is a work of stark insights and brilliantly deployed multiple perspectives. It differs from his other books, however, in that, although its two principal characters are black Africans, very little of the story is set in Sub-Saharan Africa, but is polarized rather between two distant locations: the East Coast of America and the Muslim Maghreb. This geographical breadth involves Armah in a considerable feat of balance, which he is not uniformly successful in maintaining. The problem is not so much one of physical, as of moral equi-

39

librium. For, although the plot is brought to a climax in the torrid vastness of the Saharan wastes, the ethical judgments brought to bear on it derive from America in the years of racial confrontation.

The book opens in Laccryville, the bedraggled capital of a newly independent Arab republic, a rather thin disguise for Algiers. The dilapidation of the city is evoked, but more pertinently the degradation of the population, reduced it would seem to begging an odd dinar from every passing stranger. Among these is Solo, a refugee from one of the Portuguese territories, who has fled here for safety after an abortive attempt to abet the guerilla forces in his own country. Solo is tortured by a sense of failure which is heightened by the evident futility of the revolutionary legacy around him, a point poignantly expressed by a *mutilé de guerre* he meets in the hospital library: 'Who gained? that is what I want to know. Who won?' (p. 24). Saddened by such reflections, Solo is left with a niggling dilemma, common to so many of Armah's characters: how to bear his failure, his contradiction with integrity.

Into this bleak environment wander two improbable creatures, exiles in a different sense. These are Modin Dofu, a gentle, soft-mannered Ghanaian, and Aimée, his lean and restless white American girlfriend. Aimée's name is chosen advisedly, for her entire nature is consumed by the need to be loved, to suck others dry, a fact which Solo soon discerns with uncanny insight. In Dofu he immediately recognizes an earlier vision of himself, a puzzled, questioning self with a desperate need to justify itself through some act of definition. But the definition he seeks is the one which Solo cannot provide: he wants to enlist in the guerilla army in Solo's home country, to become that anomalous and pathetic creature, an intellectual revolutionary. As Solo informs him with a shrug: 'I cannot help you. I went and failed.' He is condemned to watch and wait while Dofu's formal applications to enter the maquis are turned down. The lovers sit in their grimy *pension* and bicker constantly about the causes of their frustration. (Aimée has insisted on staying in what she somewhat risibly calls 'a revolutionary hotel' (p. 60); as Dofu wryly remarks, that simply means the dirtiest joint in town.) Eventually, their slender savings exhausted, they come to share Solo's own tiny flat.

The toughest strand in the novel is the intractable relationship traced out between the two Africans: the ardent young Dofu, and the older and sager Solo. They hardly speak to one another face to face, since Aimée's watchful jealousy comes like a knife between them. But then Solo gets his hands on Dofu's journal, and through his empathic reading of it their eerie dialogue commences. As Solo reads on, he discovers more of himself, yet, paradoxically, realizes precisely why he is impotent to help the writer. Dofu writes: 'There is no sanctuary. I have known periods of spiritual death when I have shut myself off from the world. There is loneliness that is a kind of death' (p. 159). And Solo, in thought, answers: 'Where he hoped to go I have already been. I had run back with a spirit broken with real arrangements, my mind howling for peace, any mediocre peace. What help had I to offer him?' (p. 83).

The axis of the novel changes, however, when it comes to Aimée. Because, for Solo, Dofu's love for his hysterically demanding mistress is a symptom of a fatal weakness. He is confirmed in this impression, not simply by the stormy futile passages of wrath he witnesses between them, but by the genesis and gradual growth of the relationship in America as evidenced by the papers in his possession. For he has access, not only to Dofu's diary, but to the disjointed, histrionic notes that Aimée herself has collected over the same period. Extracts from both of these are interpolated into Solo's own monologue, which forms the framework of the narrative. And from these jottings Solo is able to piece together bit by bit the path of their passionate mutual destruction, the neurotic demands of one exploiting ruthlessly the loving-kindness of the other.

Aimée is not merely demanding however; she is also frigid. Her rapturous response to Dofu is partly gratitude for his being the first man able to arouse her. And this frigidity is construed as but one aspect of the sexual illness of white America. Professor Jefferson, the Africanist scholar who takes a patronizing interest in the young Dofu on his arrival in the States, is impotent. Consequently it is left to the abashed and confused student to satisfy his nymphomaniac wife. When the professor discovers the betrayal, he comes after the copulating couple with a loaded shotgun, and dispatches Dofu to hospital with multiple wounds. Such incidents would be palatable if they were sprinkled with the slightest spice of humour. Of humour in this sense – generous, forgiving humour – however, the American scenes are almost innocent. The racial imbalance is all too obvious. Naita, Dofu's black secretary girlfriend, turns out to be a tender and expert lover. Dofu himself seems to be gifted with almost endless virility. With increasing disdain he blunders through this sexual Disneyland, servicing females in every direction. Bereft of the self-respect he so earnestly seeks, he is left to play out the role of the black buck familiar to Ralph Ellison's 'Invisible Man', but with little of the latter's perspicacity or panache.[5]

The Dofu we meet in the American sequences seems to have little in common with the haunted, sensitive creature which Solo later encounters. Here instead we have a weak, vain, vacillating youth playing out extravagant adventures because they are there, rather than in any joyful sense of self-discovery. His social reflexes have all the gaucherie one finds portrayed, with all too little irony, in John Pepper Clark's *America, Their America*.[6] A direct parallel, of course, is impossible, because one is fiction, the other autobiography. But what they do share is a certain pinched emotional tone, a sullen bragging at victories won at the expense of white hosts, on account of being lacking in either charity or self-knowledge. It is difficult to square this Dofu, albeit younger, with the delicately contemplative creature manifested in the more introspective passages in the journals, or to believe that Solo, whose faculty of self-doubt amounts to total paralysis, should see anything of himself in him.

In criticizing the novel, therefore, we have a problem. The moral focus, which is so finely tuned to the subtlest shades of moral consciousness of Solo's world, seems incapable of illuminating the depths of Dofu's American predicament. Moreover, though there is an undeniable causal connection between these two phases, at times the American portions do appear to be awkwardly integrated into the whole. Armah attempts to relate the relationship with Aimée to Solo by paralleling it with a relationship he himself had previously experienced with a white girl in Lisbon. But Solo's Sylvia is another thing altogether: a flower-like waif who succumbs to the pressure of her own society in leaving him, rather than hurt either him or her friends. One has the impression that she would be incapable of destroying anything or anybody. Indeed Solo himself admits that the parallel is weak: 'The American girl, for some reason I could not precisely grasp just then, had reminded me sharply of Sylvia. And yet, thinking of her, I realized that she was not at all like Sylvia' (p. 62). What the elusive 'reason' for the mental connection is never becomes apparent.

There is, of course, one very blatant connection: both Aimée and Sylvia are white. And, despite the 'inhibiting traces' of his love for Sylvia, it becomes increasingly evident that Solo regards this as being the source of all her failings. Indeed, there are moments when he talks of the mere fact of attachment to a white woman as if it were part of a larger racial betrayal. Describing the European mistress of Jorge Manuel, the mulatto director of the Bureau of the People's Union of Congheria, he asks 'What is her species of love but the same ancient white hatred of Africa, taking rotten form in her dry, decayed body?' (p. 229). Again, of both Dofu's love and his own, he agonizes, 'What is the root of this fatal attraction, this emotional fixity drawing us to these daughters of our white death?' (p. 230).

For Solo, then, the price which Dofu must pay for this ill-advised alliance is his own self-destruction. This sentiment is prominently endorsed by the novel's denouement. Tired with the constant delays, Aimée and Dofu decide to trek across the desert so as to enter the maquis by the back door. This leads them into the heart of the unpoliced Sahara region. Realizing the uselessness of the expedition, Dofu pleads with Aimée to turn back. She, frightened at the thought of the public ridicule with which their failure will be greeted, persuades him to continue. Eventually, they are picked up by a gang of marauding OAS terrorists. Aimée is forced to watch Dofu's torture and castration, before she herself is ravished and released, leaving Dofu to bleed to death in the desert. Irrationally she returns with Manuel's mistress to accuse Solo, and demand her notebooks. When he refuses to hand them back she devastates his room. His reaction is characteristic of his harsher assessments: 'I have never seen humans look so predatory', he says (p. 269).

The implication would seem to be that Aimée has lured Dofu on to his death, a conclusion which picks up clues dropped throughout the novel. Yet there is a softer note in Solo's voice, a mood which carries us back to the mournful, vulnerable personality suggested by the opening sequences of his narrative. In his sense of the loss of Dofu's presence, the feeling that with his death something has gone out of himself: there we have a moment of authentic elegy. This retrospective tenderness balances the bitterness, holds it in check, so that we are left with a final impression, not of stridency, but of pathos.

Yet the harsh undercurrent cannot be ignored because there are occasions on which it threatens to undermine the whole novel. One becomes increasingly aware that one is faced with a dialectic which would force all of the characters in the work into irreconcilable camps. Indeed Solo, whose voice is the most insistently hard, suggests such a scheme when he says 'Only one issue is worth our time: how to end the oppression of the African, to kill the European beasts of prey, to remake ourselves, the elected servants of Europe and America'. The answer to oppression is simply segregation, a political premiss which seems to underlie the whole book. As such the proposition is purely political, and does not concern us critically. Where the polemic interferes with the art is the point at which political segregation becomes segregation of sympathy. Armah is not humanly affected by his white characters since he is interested only to mark them out as agents of destruction. Thus Aimée, for instance, is almost an allegorical figure: she exists simply to demonstrate the rapacious main chord of her personality. The other white characters are distinctly shadowy, flitting around Dofu and torturing his spirit: they have no other function. From where in the book does this kind of distortion receive its inspiration?

A great deal of the earlier Dofu sequences are concerned with a radical criticism of America. In one notable episode Dofu visits the college refectory for breakfast, where he meets a Republican-minded fellow student called Mike. Mike is so brimming over with his complacent sense of the all-sufficiency of his country's way of life that he insists on squatting next to him and reading out at length from a Thanksgiving Day editorial from one of the Sunday newspapers, the headline from which – 'Why Are We So Blest?' – gives the novel its title. The sheer dexterity of the parody of its swelling apologetics suggests strongly the way it must be taken. In it the element of flatulence, of sheer deception in the self-defensive rhetoric of white America, is ruthlessly exaggerated and hence debunked. The fact which riles Dofu is that the vision of American life here proposed is obsessively, wilfully, exclusive of all that might threaten its vision of paradise gained: 'Anyone who can write a whole article on Thanksgiving and leave out the mass murder of the so-called Indians is a street-corner hustler, nothing better' (p. 99). Mike's answer is glib and straightforward: they are outside the scope of the article. When Dofu asks what place the struggling black masses have in this idyll, Mike replies with a model of the social universe derived from the Greeks:

We took their savage paradise and made it complex. It has two poles now, and many gradations and permutations in between. It's got heavens – and hells, as you say – built into it. After all it wouldn't be Graeco-Christian if it didn't. There's Olympus. Below that there are the plains of mediocrity. Then Tartarus. You must agree that's a much superior arrangement to just a simple paradise. (p. 100)

Dofu's reaction to these sentiments is tight-lipped and curt, but he is clearly disturbed by them. Shortly after this he vomits, and in his nausea the headline 'Why Are We So Blest?' keeps on running through his head like an idiotic refrain. His sense of dislocation here is due to the fact that Mike, in his apathetic blundering, has touched a sore spot. Dofu himself is increasingly worried by the anomaly of his position as one who, having been drawn into a metropolitan centre of supposed learning, will eventually be sent back to exploit his advantages over his people. Remarks to this effect smother the earlier passages in his journals, for instance this:

Those who stay in the prosperous areas intellectually, emotionally, psychologically, totally are not lonely ... The price they pay for not being lonely, however, is that they suffer the crudest forms of manipulation, mortification, planned ignorance ... Those who shift from the prosperity, can hope to escape some of these cruder forms of manipulation. But the price they pay is loneliness. (p. 33)

It is in an attempt to relieve this fundamental sense of isolation that Dofu cultivates Aimée's friendship, and hence, by implication, his own destruction. For him, however, and for Solo reading the journal, this represents a compromise of all that is finest within him. In his commentary, Solo amplifies the references to salvation and damnation: 'the blessed wave us in front of the damned. – We the desperate, are made symbols of hope. Filled with the stupid, puffed-up pride of the impotent, we acquiesce' (p. 108). Dofu and Solo both see themselves as members of a distinct class, a set of individuals Solo himself calls 'assimilators', torn from their roots and condemned to a life of solitary self-communion, eternally eating themselves up with the regret of their self-betrayal.

It is evident here that both Dofu and Solo subscribe to a certain historical and political case, which may be expressed in the form of a loose syllogism:

1 The influence of white civilization on African people has been, and must perforce ever be, entirely corrosive.

2 We, the *évolués*, have been induced into a position of acute dependence on the white world.

3 We therefore owe it to ourselves and our people, to destroy this dependence, by force if necessary.

The minor premiss in this argument corresponds fairly closely to the theories of neo-colonialism advanced by francophone thinkers such as the Martiniquan psychiatrist, Frantz Fanon.[7] But the major premiss, with its outright and total dismissal of any recognition of European worth, comes, I would suggest, from a different source. It is a seminal proposition of extreme black American apologetics, especially of that brand of it which flourished in the years of racial confrontation in the early sixties. And the conclusion of the syllogism, the invocation to violence, is strongly redolent of the aims of radical sects such as the Black Muslim Movement.

It will be instructive here, I think, to take note of the period in which Armah's own period of residence in America fell. The years between 1959 and 1965 were years of crisis for the Black Movement, the years of the Kennedy and Johnson administrations, the Civil Rights Movement, and Black Islam. To a politically minded student, fresh from Nkrumaist Ghana, the appeal must have been irresistible. The notion that black salvation could only be sought in dogged separation was basic to much of the most challenging thinking of that time. It has a long and respectable history in black polemics, going back ultimately to the writings of Marcus Garvey, and became a cornerstone of the Black Muslim Movement. Garvey had sought to apply it to the planned return in glory of the Negro race, to their African motherland, the Black Muslims to their demand for a Black Zion in the southern States. For Armah, it seems to have been adopted as a basis for an analysis of the contemporary African situation itself, and, by extension, the global confrontation between the races.

One can best, I think, illustrate Armah's relationship in this respect to the Afro-American movement by examining where he stands in relation to that highly ambivalent figure, James Baldwin. With the mellow Baldwin, the compassionate humanist with his conviction that black Americans must work out their destiny by persuading white men to come to terms with themselves, that, in Baldwin's own words, 'the murder must be understood', Armah has almost nothing in common. Of the occasional fire-and-brimstone Baldwin, the impassioned preacher, however, there are, in this book, many echoes. Listen to this from *My Dungeon Shook*: 'this is the crime of which I accuse my countrymen, that they have destroyed hundreds and thousands of lives and do not know it and do not want to know it'.[8] If you substitute the word Europe in the first part of that sentence, then you have Solo or Dofu at their bitterest.

The only question which remains is whether these torn characters can be seen as subscribing to the conclusion of the syllogism itself, namely, the sacred efficacy of violence. The drab and hopeless picture drawn by Solo at the beginning of the novel of post-revolutionary Algeria would seem to negate this possibility. Indeed the question aired by the war cripple, 'who gained?' which hangs like a murky cloud over the entire work, appears to be a direct challenge to it. An eight-year war with France has brought the Algerians neither prosperity nor self-respect. In this light, I would contend that the many references in Dofu's diary to the urgency of conflict must be seen as suggestive of a prolonged inner struggle of mental emancipation rather than a call to arms.

NOTES

1. All references in this chapter are to the Heinemann (African Writers Series, 1974) edition of *Why Are We So Blest?*.
2. Cf. Ernest Hemingway, *Green Hills of Africa*, New York, Charles Scribner's Sons, 1953; Saul Bellow, *Henderson the Rain King*, London, Weidenfeld & Nicholson, 1939; Paul Theraux, *Fong and the Indians*, Boston, Houghton Mifflin, 1969.
3. From *Ethiopiques*, Paris, Editions de Seuil, 1956.
4. Cf. John Pepper Clark, *America, Their America*, London, Heinemann, 1964.
5. Cf. Ralph Ellison, *The Invisible Man*, New York, Random House, 1952.
6. Clark, op. cit.
7. For an adumbration of this argument, see Frantz Fanon, *Peau Noire, Masques Blancs*, Paris, Editions de Seuil, 1952; also *Les Damnés de la Terre*, Paris, Editions de Seuil, 1961.
8. James Baldwin, *The Fire Next Time*, New York, The Dial Press, 1963, p. 19.

De origen africano, soy cubano: African Elements in the Literature of Cuba

Femi Ojo-Ade

INTRODUCTION

The fact of the Cuban revolution has often overshadowed the presence and importance of the African factor in Cuban culture. The fierce nationalism involved has naturally helped to play down the particularity and authenticity of this major African contribution. The researcher's task is not made any easier by the concept of Cuban 'criollo' culture: the island is presented as a melting-pot, a crucible of cohesive components which have been so modified that it would be almost impossible to analyse their distinctive elements. None the less, certain facts are undeniable: African slaves were transported to the canefields of Cuba as early as 1517 and, until late in the nineteenth century, the African element constituted some 50 to 60 per cent of the population.[1]

As a result of the work of scholars such as Fernando Ortiz,[2] a Euro-Cuban who has devoted most of his life to the study of the black presence in Cuba, Afro-Cuban[3] culture has come to be given its rightful place in the edification of 'lo cubano'. Cuban writers and scholars, even those with no visible African ancestry,[4] now readily accept this fact, as Angel Augier does here:

> The negro contribution to 'cubanidad' has not been negligent [sic].
> Apart from his immense energy, which made possible the economic incorporation of Cuba to world civilization, and besides his pugnacious will-power to attain freedom, which paved the way for national independence, his cultural influence can be observed in food and cookery, vocabulary, speech-patterns, oratory, amorosity ... but, above all, in three manifestations of 'cubanidad': in the arts, religion and the tone of collective emotivity.[5]

To that one may add the words of a major figure in Cuban letters, Nicolás Guillén:

> The African element in this land is so profound, and so many essential currents are found in our well-irrigated social hydrography that it would be the work of a miniaturist to decipher the hieroglyphics.[6]

And, finally, a statement by another Cuban, Lydia Cabrera:

> One cannot understand our people without knowing the Negro.[7]

What all these writers have stressed, in short, is that an evaluation of the Cuban cultured entity would not be complete without the African element. In other words, in spite of the disadvantages of being uprooted from their homeland, and the machinations of the slave-masters, the Afro-Cubans maintained their culture. Naturally, this transplanted culture has not remained static. It has evolved over the years. Certain elements have been kept while others have been discarded or modified. Fula, Mandongo, Bambara, Yoruba, Arara, Mina, Bantu, Calabar, all those various African ethnic groups have subsisted in their new environment. Life and literature bear their indelible mark, especially that of the Yoruba, the most significant of the Afro-Cuban groups.

ORAL LITERATURE

African literature was originally oral and the most traditional manifestation of this literature is in religious ceremonies. For the African, and his Afro-Cuban progeny, religion is the essence of life. The concomitancy of religion and life has been well explained by scholars such as Bolaji Idowu. Without religion, man cannot exist. 'Religion in essence is the means by which God as Spirit and man's essential self communicate.'[8] Life cannot be divided into the 'real' and the 'unreal', the secular and the sacred; the past, the present, and the future are intimately related and man's experiences on earth, as well as material objects, have meaning only in relationship to elements of the other world, the world of Olorun, the Supreme Deity, and the Orisha, the deities. Esu, Ifa, Obatala, Oduduwa, Yemoja, Sango, Ogun, etc., are major figures of the cosmos. The Afro-Cuban crossed the ocean with his religion, and his gods. His oral literature consisted of ceremonies for these divinities. Stories, myths, and legends of African origin were passed on from generation to generation; they were marked by African phonetic practices, vocabulary, expressions, and tonality. Though translated into Spanish, the original rhythm was retained. The ancestral tradition was maintained in ritual songs, songs of the liturgy, various ceremonial songs and dances. The drum, the vehicle for transmitting messages and an instrument filled with symbolic importance, came to serve the Afro-

Cuban as a means of attaining the zenith of emotivity in worship, and when the literature came to be set down in writing the rhythm of the drum could be felt in the very words of the poet. Indeed, oral literature has greatly influenced all the literature of Cuba.

WRITTEN LITERATURE: POETRY

Antecedents

As for written literature, it would be inexact to claim that no Negro-African type of writing existed before the advent of the famous negrist writers of the mid-1920s. Several anthologies contain anonymous poems and 'cantos' from the early slave period until the nineteenth century. Though rather simple in style and structure, their rhythm and use of tonality (the origin of the onomatopoeic turn in Cuban letters), have markedly influenced the negrist verses of the twentieth century.

> Piqui, piquimbín,
> piqui, piquimbín
> tumba, muchacho,
> yama bo y tambó.
> Tambó ta brabbo.
> Tumba, cajero.
> Jabla, mula.
> Piqui, piquimbín,
> piqui, piquimbín.
> Pa, pa, pa, pracá,
> prácata, pra, pa.
> Cucha, cucha mi bo.[9]

The above 'canto' mixes the sound of the drum (tumba) with the noise of the mule's feet, the dancing of the boy with the movement of the mule. Rhythm, repeated forms, are elements found in latter negrist poets. The very nature of the 'cantos' collected in the anthologies goes a long way to assert the everlasting presence of Africa in Cuba's cultural manifestations. 'Canto congo de cabildo para tres tambores', 'Canto funeral', etc., found in Guirao's book, underscore the fact that songs

> constitute a rich heritage of all Africa. Africans are always singing; and in their singing and poetry, they express themselves: all the joys and sorrows of their hearts, and their hopes and fears about the future, find outlet. Singing is always a vehicle conveying certain sentiments of truth. When they are connected with rituals, they convey the faith of worshippers from the heart – faith in Deity, belief in and about Divinities, assurance and hopes about the present and with regard to the hereafter.[10]

As we shall soon see, musicality is an essential part of the negrist poetry.

49

The Negrist Movement

Interestingly enough, the first partisans of the Negrist Movement in Cuba, mostly Euro-Cubans, did not cultivate 'lo africano' through the impact of Afro-Cuban antecedents. Cuban Negrism, comparable to Haitian Indigenism and the American Harlem Renaissance, owed its inception to the German philosophy of Oswald Spengler and to Leo Frobenius. Europe was disillusioned after the First World War. Africa was being 'discovered' by those interested in exoticism and primitivism. Also, a few genuine humanists like Frobenius – although not even they were devoid of paternalism, gratuitous optimism, and outright idealism – concluded that white civilization could learn a lot from Africa.

The Cuban Negrists opened their eyes and found right in their own country what Frobenius travelled to Africa to find. They studied the Negro, wrote about him, about his way of life and his ancestral home in 'Guinea'. Alliteration, assonance, rhythmic repetition, and onomatopoeia, these are the basic elements of the poetry. Three poets stand out: Ramón Guirao, José Tallet, and Alejo Carpentier from whom these examples are given:

–Guirao, 'Bailadora de Rumba':

Bailadora de guaguancó,	(Rumba dancer,
piel negra,	black-skinned girl,
tersura de bongó	purity of the bongo.
Agita la maraca de su risa	With laughter on her face,
con los dedos de leche	she shakes the maraca
de sus dientes.	with her young fingers,
Pañuelo rojo	her white teeth shining in the sun.
–seda–,	Red handkerchief
bata blanca	–silk–
–almidón–,	white shoe
recorren el trayecto	–starch–,
de una cuerda	enthralled by an Afro-Cuban rhythm)
en un ritmo afrocubano[11]	

–Tallet, 'La Rumba':

Zumba mamá, la rumba y tambó
mabimba, mabomba, bomba y bombó.
Chaci, chaqui, chaqui, charaqui.
Chaqui, chaqui, chaqui, charaqui.[12]

–Carpentier, 'Liturgia':

La Potencia rompió,	(The power is destroyed,
¡yamba! ó!,	Olorun be praised!
Retumban las tumbas	The drums are beating
en casa de Ecué.	and the dead are awake
El Juego firmó,	in Babaluwaye's house.
¡yamba ó!,	The cult leaders confirmed it,

con yeso amarillo	Praise be to Thee, Olorun o!,
en la puerta fambá	with yellow cast
El gayo murió,	on the doorframe.
¡yamba ó!	The cock died,
en el rojo altar	Olorun be praised!,
del gran Obatalá.[13]	on the red altar
	of the great Obatala.)

In the above poems we note briefly: (1) the use of African words: *guaguancó* (rumba in Cuba, reminiscent of the Yoruba, *gangan*, a type of drum); *bata*, shoe (same word as in Yoruba; in the latter language, *bàtá*, a type of drum, word used in other poems of the same mode); *¡yamba ó!*, God be praised (used by the Cuban Nañigó; *o!* a very common expression among Africans, used in an emphatic way, to show surprise, excitement, etc.; (2) onomatopoeia, especially in the poems of Tallet; (3) the sound of drums and other percussion instruments, worked into poems; (4) African divinities named: Obatala, vice-regent of Olorun (God), god of purity delegated by Olorun to finish the task of earthly creation. Elsewhere in these writers' poems, we find gods such as Sango, Esu, Ifa, etc.[14] The liturgy of santería, the religion of the Yoruba (Cuban Lucumí), is at the root of Carpentier's poem; (5) an African style, marked by repetition and a statement-response format, recalling in a way the Yoruba chants, like *iwi egúngún*, *ìjálá*, and *rárà*, genres of oral poetry used to sing the praise of divinities and individuals.

It should be noted that the negrist writing of Carpentier, Guirao, and others, lacks depth and, at times, sincerity. The most significant affinity their works have with Africa is in rhythm and it is no coincidence that many poems have the word 'rumba' in their title.[15] Words representing specific musical instruments and dances also abound: bongó, tambor, conga, maraca, marímbula (instruments); columbia, bembé, candombe, rumba (dances). The 'negro bembón' (thick-lipped Negro), that is, the Afro-Cuban protagonist of this poetry, is presented from the exterior, his physical attributes are dwelt upon, with particular emphasis upon his sexual prowess and practices, and his lack of seriousness. Indeed, the impression one gets from reading much of this poetry is that African dances are mainly sexually oriented. Carpentier and others resemble spectators surprised by their discoveries at a foreign ceremony, although it should be mentioned that they at times achieve an authentic rhythm reminding one of the eloquent voice of African percussion instruments, a feeling of the ancestral and its powerful influence.

Nicolas Guillén

To experience the authentic voice of Afro-Cuban poetry, one need only open the pages of any of the many collections of poetry of Nicolás Guillén, perhaps the most important writer in Cuba today.[16] In Guillén one finds sincere human emotions and profound consciousness of the African heritage. To the body created by others he has provided a heart and a soul. He is 'the only poet of this [negrist] group for whom the negro theme was neither a form, nor simply a particular theme, but the generating centre of all his creative activity'.[17]

And as the poet himself clearly states:

I deny art that only sees in the Negro a coloured motif and not an interesting human theme. Without doubt, the negro theme offers plastic qualities of the first order to the painter, extraordinary rhythmic elements to the musician and new values to the language. But let us not forget that there are millions of Negroes struggling in the most terrible slavery . . . All is not tambor, macumba, rumba, voudou . . .[18]

The poet resembles the African griot, depository of a culture; he is at once narrator, actor, dancer, a bird singing of the past, living the present and looking forward to, predicting, the future; a spirit spanning the cosmos, the heart-beat of the nation. Guillén is proud of his ancestory. He possesses the unique perspicacity and aloneness (not loneliness) necessary for attaining this lucidity.

> Yoruba soy, lloro en yoruba lucumí.
> Como soy un yoruba de Cuba,
> quiero que hasta Cuba suba mi llanto yoruba,
> que suba el alegre llanto yoruba
> que sale de mí.
> Yoruba soy,
> cantando voy,
> llorando estoy,
> y cuando no soy yoruba,
> soy congo, mandinga, carabalí. ('Son número 6')[19]

> (I am a Yoruba, I cry in Cuban Yoruba.
> Since I am a Yoruba from Cuba,
> I want my Yoruba tears to spread to Cuba,
> I want the happy Yoruba tears
> emanating from me to spread, to rise.
> I am a Yoruba,
> I am singing, continually,
> I am crying,
> and when I am not a Yoruba,
> I am from the Congo, I am from Calabar.)

The declaration of ancestry is not made merely with words. In 'El canto negro', the feelings are captured in the rhythm, in the sounds and phonemes, in the onomatopoeic turnings, in the style. The Negro becomes one with the rhythm, the song, the music. Everything is saturated by the melodious syncopation of his Africanity. The pulsating sound of the drums fills the air.

> ¡Yambambó, yambambó!
> Repica el congo solongo,
> repica el negro bien negro;
> congo solongo del Songo
> baila, yambó sobre un pie.
> Mamatomba,
> serembe cuserembá.
>
> El negro canta y se ajuma,
> el negro se ajuma y canta,
> el negro canta y se va...
>
> Tamba, tamba, tamba, tamba,
> tamba del negro que tumba.[20]

To this one may add the verses of the 'Canción del bongó'[21] in which the unmistakable sound of the talking drum is present. The proud Afro-Cuban – *el negro bien negro*, the real Negro, the Negro conscious of his Negro-ness – remembers his faraway home, sings about it, dances about it, worships his ancestral gods, but is bent upon asserting his rights in his new home. Guillén feels and communicates the sentiments and idiosyncracies of the Cuban Negro and mulatto. There is, in his poems, no emphasis on the folkloric *per se*; the cultural is made social, political, human. A poem, 'Sensemayá', full of onomatopoeia, depicts the religious practices of the Afro-Cuban. The poems of *Sóngoro Cosongo*, noted for their 'jitanjáforas' – words without specific meaning invented by the artist and used for their suggestive power – evoke the spiritual and mysterious elements of Africa. Other poems by Guillén present 'una voz antigua y de hoy/moderna y bárbara' (see *West Indies Ltd*), a harmonious blend of the past and the present.

Marcelino Arozarena

Even more than Guillén, Arozarena shows a profound knowledge of African culture, especially in his collection of poetry, *Canción negra sin color* (1966). He is well versed in Yoruba liturgy. His rhythm is authentically African; in 'Carnaval de Santiago', he evokes a traditional ceremony in which evil is driven out of a patient, using the rhythm of the drum to mark the proceedings, from the subdued beginning to the culmination in a crescendo of sounds when the objective of the ceremony is achieved. Then, the poet turns the whole ceremony into a socially symbolic art of driving out the oppressor. Yemaja, Ogun, and other gods are positively evoked in Arozarena's works. The sublimity, absent from the poetry of others before him, is restored to African religious feeling.

PROSE

Cuban prose, not as widely practised as poetry, has less African flavour than the other genre. The most famous writer in the Africanist vein is Alejo Carpentier whose novel, *¡Ecué-Yamba-O!* (1933), has been hailed as an authentic illustration of Africanity in Cuba. However, a close study of the novel, the biography of an imaginary black Cuban, Menegildo Cué, from his birth to his murder in the hands of a rival for the affection of his woman, reveals that Carpentier treats his subject exclusively as an outsider. Descriptions of African religious and cultural practices abound and the novelist lists a paraphernalia of objects and gods used in native medicine. Many gods are carefully described. We are introduced several times into the household of the 'doctor', Old Berúa:

> A table covered with coarse cloth held a veritable paraphernalia of divinities and instruments. The Christian images, to start with, freely enjoyed the splendour of a secret life, unknown by the non-initiated. At the centre, on a ritual drum, rose Obatala, the crucified, imprisoned in a network of interwoven beads. At his feet, Yemaya, diminutive Virgen de la Regla, was imprisoned in a crystal bottle. Sango, under the aegis of Santa Barbara, second element of the trinity of the major Orisha, brandished a golden sabre.[22]

But the drawn-out descriptions lack positivity. Carpentier's stand throughout the novel is, that African religion is superstition, and her medicine, mere speculation. Menegildo, the hero, is the quintessence of the black stereotype, strong, sexually competent, simple, and simplistic, imbued with hereditary rhythm. The novelist himself owns up to a lack of intimate knowledge and comprehension of the subject of his text:

> In a period marked by a great interest in Afro-Cuban folklore ... I wrote a novel – *¡Ecué-Yamba-O!* – whose characters were Negroes of the rural class of that time. I must observe that I grew up on the Cuban countryside in contact with sons of Black peasants; that, later, very interested in the practice of santería, and of ñañiguismo, I attended innumerable ritual ceremonies. With that documentation I wrote a novel that was published in Madrid, in 1933, at the height of European primitivism. Now then: after twenty years of investigation about the sincretic realities of Cuba, I realized that the profound, the essential, the universal of the world that I had claimed to depict in my novel had remained out of my reach ...[23]

That is the price that the avowed outsider often has to pay.

Where Carpentier failed, Lydia Cabrera[24] has succeeded. Not only is she an ethnologist; she is also a sociologist, a psychologist, a religious student of Afro-Cuban culture, a totally devoted follower of Africanity as manifested in Cuba. It was only after a very serious study of the culture, achieved through an intimacy with old Negroes who, naturally, are the closest to the original culture, that Lydia Cabrera wrote her famous short stories. She studied the language of the people and even prepared a dictionary of Yoruba (Lucumí) language. Her stories are filled with episodes similar to those still told in Africa. They reflect the psyche of the Afro-Cuban, an anti-intellectual animist vision, an identification with nature, and a strong belief in the will of the gods. In *¿Por qué?*, each story is a question about an element of African culture. 'El chivo hiede' – [Why] the goat stinks; 'El tiempo combate con el sol y la luna consuela a la tierra' – [Why] time fights the sun and the moon consoles the earth; 'El cangrejo no tiene cabeza' – [Why] the crab has no head, etc.; each of these stories discusses an aspect of mythology and they remind the reader of the African night-stories, told by the elders under the full moon.

Divinities are constantly present in Lydia Cabrera's stories, either as determinants of man's destiny or as protagonists themselves. She knows the exact personality and traits of each god. Rituals and ceremonies are not described as mere episodes but as essential parts of the plot and the lives of the characters, whose duty it is to praise the Orisha, to be in their good grace and to avoid arousing their wrath. The writer has achieved a genuine syncretization of the Afro-Cuban culture which, as was earlier stated, is made up of several diverse ethnic parts from Africa. The characters of her studies have not only been successful in merging their different cultural beliefs together, but have also achieved a fusion between their own religion and Catholicism.[25]

CONCLUSIONS

In the final analysis, it is this process of *sincretismo* – the conciliation of divergent parts, the fusion of opposing cultural elements into a harmonious whole – that stands out in any study of Cuban literature.[26] Each writer in the negrist mode views Africanity, not as a goal in itself, but as a means of realizing, in conjunction with the Spanish element, the true mestize culture of Cuba. Africa is a source to be remembered, not a place to be returned to, for that would constitute an act of cowardice and useless daydreaming. Africa is used as an inspiration, a means of assimilation, of a fusion, so that a true Cuban society can be effectuated. The African elements cannot be separated and viewed separately without placing them in the Cuban context, and without taking cognizance of the Spanish element.

'Lo cubano', neither white nor black, neither Spanish nor African but derived from both white and black, something particular, self-asserting, nationalistic, is what the Cuban scholar, Fernando Ortiz, has called 'la transculturación'. 'The national synthesis of Cuba, affirms Angel Augier, has been realized with the thesis of the Spanish element and the antithesis of the African.'[27]

So much is also stated in the works of Guillén: 'Yo/hijo de América/ hijo de ti y de Africa' (I/son of America/your son and Africa's son: the poet is addressing Spain).

The same is asserted by a younger poetess, Nancy Morejón:

Ya nunea más imaginé el camino a Guinea.
¿Era a Guinea? ¿A Benin? ¿Era a Madagascar? ¿O a Cabo Verde?
-Trabajé mucho más ...

Aquí construí un mundo. ('Mujer negra')[28]

The song is inspired by Africa but is sung for the good of Cuba, celebrating work done by the slave in Cuba, and Cuba's striving to attain her freedom and humanness. Hope is in the future in Cuba, and the road back to Africa is forgotten. There is no general identification with Africa here; for, if it is true that Africa lives on in the Cuban spirit, it is no less true that the Cuban nation has to determine its own destiny. Africa spells the past, Cuba represents the future. Cuban spirit is unmistakably mestizo, and the Afro-Cuban poet can rightly affirm: 'My roots are in Africa, but I am a Cuban to the core.'[29]

NOTES

All translations, except where otherwise stated, are the author's.
1. Several texts deal at length with the history of Cuba. See, for example, Rafael Fermoselle-López, 'The Black in Cuba: A Bibliography', *Caribbean Studies*, XII, 3, October 1972, pp. 103–12.
2. Fernando Ortiz, *Hampa afro-cubana: los negros brujos*, 1906; *El engaño de las razas*, La Habana, 1945.
3. In the present chapter, Afro-Cuban is used in the sense of that which is of African origin in Cuba. No attempt is made to impose the African element upon others. It should be noted that, to some critics, the term 'Afro-Cuban' implies some form of superiority of the African element.
4. For example, Ramón Guirao and Salvador Bueno.
5. Angel Augier, *Nicolás Guillén*, tomo I, La Habana, Universidad Central de las Villas, 1965, p. 99.
6. Nicolás Guillén, *Obra poética*, tomo I, La Habana, Instituto cubano del libro, 1972, p. 114.
7. Lydia Cabrera, *El monte*, Miami, Florida, Rema Press, 1968, p. 9.
8. E. Bolaji Idowu, *African Traditional Religion, a Definition*, Orbis Books, Maryknoll, N.Y., 1973, p. 75.
9. Ramón Guirao, *Orbita de la poesía afrocubana*, La Habana, 1970, p. 3.

10. Idowu, op. cit., p. 85.
11. Guirao, op. cit., p. 55.
12. ibid., p. 65
13. ibid., p. 77.
14. For a thorough study of African religion in Africa and Cuba, see Lydia Cabrera, op. cit., and E. Bolaji Idowu, *Olodumare*, Longman, London, 1966.
15. Other examples, apart from those already quoted are: 'Rumba' (Emilio Ballagas), 'Rumba' (Alfonso Hernández Catá), 'Rumba de la negra Pancha' (José Antonio Portuondo), etc., all taken from Guirao's anthology.
16. Nicolás Guillén, *Motivos de son*, 1930; *Sóngoro Cosongo*, 1931; *West Indies Ltd*, 1934 (among others).
17. Cintio Vitier, *Cincuenta años de poesiá cubana, 1902–1952*, p. 229.
18. Augier, op. cit., pp. 286–7.
19. Guillén, *Obra poetica*, tomo I, p. 231.
20. ibid., p. 122.
21. ibid., p. 116.
22. Alejo Carpentier, *¡Ecué-Yamba-O!*, Editorial Xanadu, 1968, p. 83.
23. In *Tientas y diferencias*, La Habana, 1966.
24. Lydia Cabrera has several works on African manifestations in Cuban culture and each is well researched and well documented: *Cuentos negros de Cuba*, 1940; *¿Por que?*, 1948; *Anagó*, 1957; etc.
25. See Hilda Pepera, *Idapo, el sincretismo en los cuentos de Lydia Cabrera*, 1971.
26. Whether such harmony exists within the larger society is being debated. Several critics, among them Cuban blacks, claim that racism does exist in Cuba, but that is not the subject of this chapter. See Carlos More, 'Le peuple noir a-t-il sa place dans la révolution cubaine?', *Présence Africaine*, 52, 4e trimestre 1964, pp. 177–230.
27. Ortiz, op. cit., p. 99.
28. In *Casa las Americas*, 88, 1975, p. 119.
29. Modification of chapter-title.

Prophet of Violence: Chester Himes

Willfried Feuser

> I am carving God in night,
> I am painting hell in white . . .
> (W. E. B. Dubois, 1899)

The 1940s, which witnessed a boom of black protest literature in the United States initiated by Richard Wright's *Uncle Tom's Children* (1938) and *Native Son* (1940) and sustained by such novels as William Attaway's *Blood on the Forge* (1941), Ann Fetry's *The Street* (1946), and William Gardner Smith's *The Last of the Conquerors* (1948), to mention but a few, also saw the emergence of Chester Himes as a major American writer – a writer, however, who like the prophet of old did not find acceptance and recognition in his own home-town.

Although Himes had published his first short stories in *Abbott's Monthly* as far back as 1932, and in *Esquire* as from 1934, his first novel, *If He Hollers Let Him Go*, did not appear until 1945. It was a fair success, albeit far from what its masterful self-analysis, its courageous probing of the racial cancer, its unity of mood and structural perfection would have led one to expect. At any rate this first success was sufficient encouragement for Himes to concentrate on the writing of his second novel, *Lonely Crusade*, published in 1947. In both novels the author had treated the theme of the black man in a hostile white industrial world; in both his black protagonist had been involved with white women. But it seems that it was the injection of a stronger dose of political analysis that inflamed critical opinion against Himes's second novel:

> Everybody disliked *Lonely Crusade*; the Blacks disliked it, the whites disliked it, the Communists ran a real assault on it, the reactionaries disliked it, the Jews disliked it, everybody.[1]

This rejection which, according to Himes, was due to the fact that he came too close to the truth, nearly broke his tough spirit and led to years of self-doubt and indecision:

Of all the hurts which I had suffered before – my brother's accident, being kicked out of college, my parents' divorce, my term in prison, and my racial hell on the West Coast – and which I have suffered since, the rejection of *Lonely Crusade* hurt me most.[2]

At that time two of his novels, *Black Sheep*, which later became *Cast the First Stone* (1952), and *The Third Generation* (1954), an American tragedy of youth and futile rebellion, were still with his agent. But the author, a man in his early forties, felt down-and-out; his marriage was breaking up, he was unable to support his wife and too proud to accept the idea of her supporting him. He held a number of insignificant, mostly menial jobs, like that of day porter at the White Plains, NY, YMCA ('a strictly Jim Crow institution at that time'):

> When I quit at the last of March, three months later, the director said I had been one of the best porters they had ever had and he hated to see me leave, but he would give me a good recommendation. I told him I was going to devote my time to writing. 'But how will you live?' he wanted to know. That was the question.[3]

Such was the pinnacle of recognition Chester Himes achieved in the United States. Never did he find out the reason 'for all the processed American idiocy, ripened artificially like canned cheese'[4] that made him a *persona non grata* in his own country, and he therefore tried to escape from it. Even as a raw youth he had felt the compulsion, nurtured by an intricate configuration of individual, familial, and racial factors, to leave the country:

> In addition I wanted to get away; I wanted to leave Cleveland and Ohio and all the United States of America and go somewhere I could escape the thought of my parents and my brother, somewhere black people weren't considered the shit of the earth. It took me forty years to discover that such a place does not exist.[5]

The first attempt 'to get away' ended in utter failure. In fact it landed the 19-year-old ex-college student in prison for armed robbery: 'I grew to manhood in the Ohio State penitentiary ...' (*QH*, p. 60). The second attempt many years later, financially buoyed by the advance payments on his two aforementioned novels and sparked off by a dramatic, drunken affair with a white socialite (later depicted as Kriss Cummings in his novel *The Primitive*, 1955) that brought him to the brink of murder, ended more successfully in Paris, among black American expatriates and some of the kingpins of the French intelligentsia. James Baldwin remembers him towering above the pygmies that were busy licking Richard Wright's boots:

> Richard and I, of course, drifted farther and farther apart – our dialogues became too frustrating and too acrid – but, from my helplessly sardonic

distance, I could only make out, looming above what seemed to be an indescribable cacophonous parade of mediocrities, and a couple of the world's most empty and pompous black writers, the tough and loyal figure of Chester Himes.[6]

After publishing one more novel in the United States and spending a few more years of purgatory in France and Spain – seedy hotel rooms, unpaid bills, and strangling money-lenders in his dreams – Chester Himes managed 'to break into the big time' with the first of a series of detective novels about Harlem, entitled *For Love of Imabelle*, which won him the 'Grand Prix de Littérature Policière' for 1958. Thus, ironically, success came to Chester Himes through his crime fiction, which he considered strictly a bread-and-butter affair. Still more ironically, it came to him through publication in a foreign tongue – the majority of the series were first published in French – and the highest praise was showered on him by renowned French writers. For Marcel Duhamel, translator of *If He Hollers Let Him Go* and editor of Gallimard's prestigious 'Série Noire', Himes is a living myth – 'Le Mythe'.[7] Jean Cocteau called *For Love of Imabelle* 'the most extraordinary novel I have read in a long time', and Jean Giono extolled it as 'a prodigious masterpiece'.[8]

One may legitimately wonder whether there is any link – ideological, artistic, or otherwise – between the two main phases in Chester Himes's literary career, that of rejection, during which he felt that if Christ were still alive, even the Bible would not find a publisher in the USA,[9] and that of recognition, achieved in a splendid apotheosis 'from cotton sacks to Cadillacs', as his characters would be likely to put it. The answer is that few black writers have shown throughout their career the same singleness of purpose, the same determination to stick to their guns, and a similar reluctance to give credit to the 'deliberate speed' of social change with regard to the Negro question in the United States; for him it is tantamount to immobilism. What he wrote in his searing, visionary political sketch, 'Prediction' (1969), is qualitatively the same as his militant expostulations in several essays written during the Second World War, from 'Now is the time! Here is the place!' (1942), to 'Negro martyrs are needed' (1944).[10] One can be sure that Himes would fully endorse Richard Wright's statement, who when asked about the danger inherent in his Parisian self-exile of losing touch with US life snapped back, 'The Negro problem in America has not changed in 300 years'.[11] Thus Chester Himes has ruggedly adhered to his over-riding preoccupation with *black protest against white oppression* (matched only by his concern with black heterosexuality) although the treatment has changed from tragedy to comedy, or outright farce. He is like a musical wizard who plays the trombone during the first part of a soirée and then, after the intermission, grabs a stuffed trumpet and treats his audience to variations on the same theme. This change of mood does not alter the author's thematic framework, nor his basic pessimism. When in the early fifties high hopes were raised for the winning of negro rights, culminating in the US Supreme Court's Desegregation Decision in 1954, and other black writers toned down the protest motif, like William Demby in *Beetlecreek* (1950), Owen Dodson in *Boy at the Window* (1951), and Richard Wright in *The Outsider* (1953), or gave it a Ghandian turn, like William Melvin Kelly in his masterful novel, *A Different Drummer* (1959), Himes turned on his protest full blast, with *The Third Generation* (1954) and – in a paroxysm of white heat – *The Primitive* (1955), although an observant reader would point out that his prison novel, *Cast the First Stone* (1952), which uses white characters, shows if not a slackening, then at least a transposition of the protest motif.

Goethe, the herald of the idea of 'world literature', once called the totality of his works 'fragments of a great confession'. In the same sense each of Chester Himes's works contains an incandescent core of autobiography, starting with his early short story 'To What Red Hell' (1934), which is based on the notorious Easter Monday fire of 1930 in the Ohio State Penitentiary. The style and technique of the 'hard-boiled' novel of a Dashiell Hammett, whose *Maltese Falcon* he read in prison, became his own, not only in his comparatively late Harlem series but to a perceptible extent also in his pre-exile novels, particularly *If He Hollers Let Him Go*. These devices were perfectly attuned to his own techniques of survival in a hostile world characterized by senseless violence: 'Two black convicts cut each other to death over a dispute as to whether Paris was in France or France in Paris' (*QH*, p. 63).

The prison scenes in Chester Himes are often reminiscent of Henri Charrière's *Papillon*. Both men were great gamblers – Chester became the syndicate boss for the gambling game among the black prisoners in Ohio State Pen – but while the Frenchman, in claiming factual depiction, seems to go off at a tangent into the realm of fabulation, the black American moves in the opposite direction. He feels that generally fiction has to be authenticated by fact. His novels, as we stated before, are veritable pages from the big book which is the story of his life, but since his autobiography appeared nearly forty years after his first published works of fiction, entire passages in it read as if they had been lifted from his novels. For Himes, facts are sacred, and even one step from the truth of his individual and social experience for him is artistic and moral treason.

Factual references to the time, place, and circumstances that led to the writing of one or the other of his novels abound in his autobiography: (Los Angeles, 1942) 'It was from the accumulation of my racial hurts that I wrote my bitter novel of protest *If He Hollers Let Him Go*' (*QH*, p. 75). (New

York, 1944) 'During that time I encountered the experiences which I later put into my novel *Pinktoes*' (ibid.).

Himes's craving for authenticity was the root cause of the paralysing ostracism he suffered after the publication of his second novel, *Lonely Crusade*. He says about the contents of the book, 'I did not record a single event that I hadn't known to happen' (*QH*, p. 101). The patriots – and they represent the majority of the populace, as Muhammad Ali discovered when he declared that he had no war with the Vietcong – were bound to resent the protagonist's enthusiastic reception of the first Japanese planes over Los Angeles after the Pearl Harbor disaster. After all, Lee Gordon mused, the Japanese might succeed where white America had failed, despite the wartime industrial boom, and despite F. D. Roosevelt's Executive Order 8802 ('There shall be no discrimination in the employment of workers in defense industries . . .'), namely, in providing him with a job:

> 'They're here!' Lee cried exultantly. 'They're here! Oh, Goddamit, they're coming. Come on, you little bad bastards! Come on and take this city!'[12]

The Communists, the author's erstwhile allies, objected to being depicted as treacherous cynics using the black masses as raw material for creating their own special type of society. In the following scene the communist leader, Rosenburg, tries to convince Lee Gordon that there is no such thing as a negro problem:

> 'The Negro problem is indivisible from the problem of the masses. You have no special problem. And Russia is the only country in the world where human rights are placed above property rights. As long as Russia stands the masses will have hope.'
> 'Not the Negro in America. Our only hope is here where Russian influence will never mean a thing.' (*LC*, p. 93)

The Jews on the other hand disliked being reminded of their own shortcomings in human relations:

> 'Of all the rotten results of racial prejudice,' Rosie said, 'anti-Semitism in a Negro is the worst.'
> 'I think the same thing about anti-Negroism in a Jew,' Lee retorted. 'With Jews being slaughtered in Europe by the hundreds of thousands, brutalized beyond comprehension, you Jews here in America are more prejudiced against Negroes than the gentiles.' (*LC*, p. 156)

His own soul brothers took exception to Himes's plea for special privileges for the black man during the initial phase of improving race relations to make equality a going concern (*LC*, p. 144). But Himes also managed to incur the wrath of a far more powerful group, Big Business:

I think that many of the critics on the big weekly reviews disliked most the characterization of the industrialist Foster, who in my book called President Roosevelt 'a cripple bastard, with a cripple bastard's sense of spite'. I had heard these words spoken in a Cleveland, Ohio, country club. Maybe the critics had heard them too – maybe that was what they most disliked, my audacity in repeating them. (*QH*, p. 101)

Of course, the author here does not just repeat naively what he hears, nor does he ever simply depict what he sees. A tape-recorder, the lifeless eye of a camera, could do the job much better. In a paper read at the University of Chicago in 1948, Chester Himes said:

> We write not only to express our experiences, out intellectual processes, but to interpret the meaning contained in them . . . Man cannot live without some knowledge of the purpose of life. If he can find no purpose in life he creates one in the inevitability of death . . . He must find the meaning regardless of the quality of his experiences. Then begins his slow, tortured progress toward truth.[13]

Foster's murderous jibe at the father of the New Deal, objectively rendered by the writer as his own contribution to truth, reveals the inner workings of a whole powerful current in American life, that of the catch-as-catch-can economic elite, bitterly resentful of any social measures for the betterment of the underprivileged masses. The German-American writer Hans Habe – before turning all-out reactionary himself – called this tendency 'Businessman-Faschismus', a term he applied to the J. F. Kennedy era when people used to sing:

> My uncle down in Texas
> Can hardly write his name.
> He signs his checks with X'es,
> They cash them just the same.[14]

In the twenty years between FDR's demise and JFK's violent exit nothing was to change, and 'my uncle down in Texas' is sure to have given a gleeful chuckle when he heard about the Houston shooting in November 1963: Chester Himes's Mr Foster is still with us. He is more alive than ever.

Despite all his reverses Chester Himes went doggedly on writing. Even after his breakthrough in Europe he still considered himself 'the lowest-paid writer on the face of the earth'.[15] But nothing could ever deter him:

> No matter what I did, or where I was, or how I lived, I had considered myself a writer ever since I'd published my first story in *Esquire* when I was still in prison in 1934. Foremost a writer. Above all else a writer. It was my salvation, and it is. The world can deny me all other employment, and stone me as an ex-convict, as a nigger, as a disagreeable and unpleasant person. But as long as I write, whether it is published or not, I'm a writer, and no one can take that away. 'A fighter fights, a writer writes', so I must have done my writing. (*QH*, p. 117)

In his novel *The Primitive* Himes depicts the black writer Jesse Robinson, author of two books, engaged in a running battle with his publishers who want him either to produce material in the plantation tradition – 'Negroes must always live happily and never die' – or protest pamphlets seething with hate. Robinson's unforgivable sin was to have tried being fair to all sides – 'take the hate but hate the compassion . . . hate the objectivity . . . guilt invites hate but hates reason . . . hates pity . . . hates forgiveness most . . . great race though . . . conquered the world . . . proves they're right. .'. Only resignation remains, 'This is the age of the great black fighters. Next century for great black writers' (*TP*, pp. 94, 116, 100). In a drunken stupor Jesse not only stabs his manuscript – a symbolic act of suicide – but also kills his white lover, paradoxically the only way open to a sable native son to gain recognition as an equal. He soliloquizes:

'End product of the impact of Americanism on one Jesse Robinson – black man. Your answer, son. You've been searching for it. *Black man kills white woman.* All the proof you need now. Absolutely incontrovertible behaviourism of a male human being. Most human of all behavior. Human beings only species of animal life where males are known to kill their females. Proof beyond all doubt. Jesse Robinson joins the human race . . .' (*TP*, p. 158)

The Third Generation, dedicated to Jean, his lovely ex-wife whom he could not support, shows Chester Himes at the peak of his creative power. It is an American psycho-drama of childhood and youth three generations after bedazzled slaves were turned into bewildered freedmen. Charles Taylor, the youngest of three brothers, is torn between a black father of unadulterated African stock, whom he respects, and a near-white mother, the descendant of house slaves, whom he adores. The whole bitter history of race relations in the United States is re-enacted in the Taylor family. Mrs Taylor's mythomania, inflamed by inordinate pride in her white Southern senator grandfather, adds a general and a US president to her pedigree for good measure. Thus fortified she lords it over her husband, the simple descendant of field-hands, whose initial competence and artistry as a blacksmith and head of the mechanical department of a southern State college in the Booker T. Washington tradition is progressively stunted, and his self-respect eroded, by his wife's constant nagging. Their terrified children have to suffer it all:

'Can't you see,' she went on, 'I want the children to have it better, not just be common pickaninnies.'
'Pickaninnies!' Her thoughtless remark cut him to the quick. 'That's better than being white man's leavings.'
She whitened with fury. It was the second time he'd slurred her parents but this time was all the more hurting because they were dead, and she revered their memory. Striking back, she said witheringly, 'You're

nothing but a shanty nigger and never will be anything else. And you would love nothing better than to have my children turn out to be as low and common as yourself.'

He jumped to his feet, shouting with rage and frustration, 'And you're a yellow bitch who thinks she's better than God Himself!'

Upstairs the children lay quiet and listened, scarcely breathing. They trembled with fear and hurt.[16]

Mrs Taylor's constant conflicts with her neighbours, both black and white, send the family on an odyssey through Georgia, Mississippi, Arkansas, Missouri, and Ohio, where Mr Taylor ends up as a janitor and an alcoholic.

Although passionately loved by his mother and protected by his father, Charles Taylor, on whom the narrative focus of the story is concentrated, quite early in life feels a morbid fascination with fate, decay, and death. During a devastating fire in the 'Patch', the black ghetto of a southern town, he comes face to face with utter rejection – a feeling which is never to leave him:

She was a young mulatto girl, dark hair hanging to her shoulder; a vague shape in a loose nightgown. There was in her posture a strange bitter forlornness more terrible than a Gorgon's head. He was too young to know that she was a whore watching the fire from morbid curiosity. He saw only the infinite loneliness of a strange lost woman in the one left house. He was ineffably drawn to her; he felt an affinity deeper than kin. He went toward her timidly, filled with the great flaming desire to serve her with his life.

'Can I help you, lady?'

She looked at him startled, then cursed. 'Git der hell away from heah an' min' yo' own bizness.'

He felt a sharp, breackish shock, turned and fled . . . deep inside he was badly hurt . . . poisoned by the strange woman's scorn . . . her rejection cut him to the heart . . . (*3rd G.*, p. 108)

When his favourite brother William is blinded in a chemical experiment, although it was on him, Charles, that their mother had called the wrath of Heaven – 'God doesn't like ugly' – Charles loses his belief in a world ordered through moral law. His sense of rejection is intensified:

He'd be lost without his brother. And he'd never again see him throughout all eternity because he was going to Hell and Will would go to Heaven. (*3rd G.*, p. 129)

Charles fails as a student, as a lover, and as a son. His oedipal condition compounded with his trauma of rejection and a sense of physical incapacity – a fall in the elevator shaft of a hotel where he was working as a busboy has left him a cripple – lead him into crime and debauchery: 'He felt the sweet acid shock of utter evil' (*3rd G.*, p. 302). His mother, although divorced from her husband a long time ago, calls on the old man for help in extricating Charles from the den of vice. Mr Taylor is stabbed to death by a pimp. The prodigal son, now sober and repentant, realizes that he has lost both parents when he sees his mother sitting stony-faced by his father's body:

> He knew then, in that instant, that she had gone back to his father; that she would belong to his father now forever. He felt as if he had been cut in two, as if a part of himself had been severed from himself forever. But at that moment it did not hurt; the hurt had not come. (*3rd G.*, p. 315)

The *leitmotif* of self-abasement and self-hatred, which is as evident here as in Jesse Robinson's methodical suicide through alcohol in *The Primitive*, has left many middle-of-the-road critics, whether white or black, disconcerted. Blyden Jackson detects 'a strange diabolism in Himes' approach to his material . . . a love of putrid matter'. He denies in particular *The Third Generation* any artistic or social relevance: 'It is just an exercise in horror, without validity as a significant interpretation of Negro, or any other kind, of life.'[17] This revulsion manifested by a well-known black critic may well be indicative of his own desperate search for social certainty and acceptance by white America. Whoever looks into an abyss without being free from vertigo does well to close his eyes and pretend that the abyss does not exist. On the other hand one feels a sneaking suspicion that a critic who lists a hard-working author's fourth published novel under the heading 'Blithe Newcomers' is either culpably ignorant or plainly malevolent. Be that as it may, Chester Himes's fictional characters are neither supermen in crime, nor is their occasional profligacy of their own making. There is, for better or for worse, a heavy environmentalist streak in Himes's conception of life and art – a tendency which is characteristic of the whole Wrightian generation – but this would not seem to detract from his competence as a writer or from his relevance as a social critic.

Himes mostly presents little people caught in something bigger than themselves, people who have not yet been able to buy their immunity from hurt like the black millionaire who used to say 'When I was a Negro . . .'. A typical example from among his characters is 'Lee Gordon, a human being, one of the cheap, weak people of the world' (*LC*, p. 365). The constant stress of being assessed less human than they feel themselves to be leaves its mark on them, the indelible 'mark of oppression'. Their hopes are evanescent, their hates pathological, and their fears constant like the ticking of a clock. There is no escape for them, not even in their dreams. Like Wright, Himes is at his psychological best in some of his dream sequences – in *The Third Generation*, *The Primitive*, and *If He Hollers Let Him Go*. His characters can speak with Job:

> When I think that my bed will console me,
> My sleep will relieve my distress,

> Then thou doest haunt me with dreams
> And horrify me with visions.
>
> Job 7: 13–14 (my translation)

Like Charles Taylor, like Jesse Robinson, Lee Gordon feels the lure of self-destruction:

> There had been that deep fascination, that tongueless call of suicide, offering not the anodyne of death, but the decadent, rotten sense of freedom that comes with being absolved of the responsibility of trying any longer to be a man in a world that will not accept you as such. (*LC*, p. 52)

This is the most deeply felt desire of all Himesian characters, *to be accepted as a man*. As Robert Jones, the protagonist of Himes's first novel, puts it:

> That's all I'd ever wanted – just to be accepted as a man – without ambition, without distinction, either of race, creed, or color; just a simple Joe walking down an American street, going my simple way, without any other identifying characteristics but weight, height, and gender.[18]

Robert Jones often hides his anxiety under a tough swagger, carrying his muscle as high as his ears, to use his own idiom. His basic desire is light-years apart from the black militancy he – and his author – are capable of. It is in fact plainly integrationist; integrationist to the point of racial self-denial; dangerously close to a trend which the young James Baldwin, himself a bewildered integrationist who felt that there was no way back since America had made him 'unfitted for the jungle or the tribe', was to denounce in one of his first essays four years later: 'The aim has now become to reduce all Americans to the compulsive, bloodless dimensions of a guy named Joe.'[19]

It is only when his astounding reservoir of goodwill towards America is exhausted, his desire for acceptance and recognition thwarted, his humanity derided, his manhood trampled underfoot, his whole being pushed to the brink of degeneracy and self-destruction, that the Himesian hero strikes back, and viciously too. Starting from this zero point of despair, Himes has evolved a theory of violence to which Frantz Fanon owes a great deal,[20] as he does likewise to his favourite writer apart from J.-P. Sartre, Richard Wright. If it is true, as Eldridge Cleaver has said, that 'the central event of our era [is] the national liberation movements abroad and the Negro revolution at home',[21] Himes may admittedly have paid scant attention to the former and to the nexus between the two but there can be no gainsaying that he was one of the first – and certainly one of the most vocal – advocates of the 'Negro revolution at home'. Intellectually he pre-dated the 'New black militancy'[22] of the mid-sixties by at least twenty years.

If, however, we go by the young Chester's crudely articulated individual revolt in the slums of Cleveland, he scores a margin of nearly forty years:

I discovered that I had become very violent. I saw a glimmer of fear and caution in the eyes of most people I encountered: squares, hustlers, gamblers, pimps, even whores. I had heard that people were saying, 'Little Katzi will kill you'. I can't say what I might have done. I swapped my .32 for a huge, old-fashioned .44 Colt frontier revolver that looked like a hand cannon and would shoot hard enough to kill a stone. I remember once being refused service at the counter of a restaurant at 105th Street and Cedar Avenue, on the very fringe of the ghetto and just two blocks from the Baptist church my father attended. I jumped to the top of the counter and kicked everything movable onto the floor – people's half-filled plates, glasses, pie bins, coffee cups, everything – and then struck the white girl behind the counter on the shoulder with my .44 caliber revolver and beat the white proprietor repeatedly across the head. The customers fled. I walked out and walked away. I was never arrested, never charged; as far as I know there was no inquiry. (*QH*, p. 47)

Himes's theory of violence, which is expected to appear in book form soon,[23] thus demonstrably has a solid grounding in practice. His practical experience comes in useful when he takes the reader on a binge through Harlem, not the Harlem of the 'New Negro' that made Claude McKay's heart throb with the spirit of communion, but a bitter, cancerous conglomeration of urban housing compounded of all the black ghettos in the USA with their fears, hates, and frustrations accumulated over centuries of oppression.

The two detectives of the Harlem series, Coffin Ed Johnson and Grave Digger Jones, aware of the impression a show of force will never fail to make in Harlem, whip out their long-barrelled, nickel-plated .38 revolvers – an outdated but conspicuous model – whenever the going gets rough.[24] Grave Digger roars 'Straighten up!', Coffin Ed, 'Count off', and if in a generous mood Grave Digger will caution his clientele by adding, 'Don't make graves'. Then hoodlums and hustlers, hep-cats and weedheads, junkies and freaks will freeze in their tracks, for the two men's reputation is formidable:

Coffin Ed had killed a man for breaking wind. Grave Digger had shot both eyes out of a man who was holding a loaded automatic. The story was in Harlem that these two black detectives would kill a dead man in his coffin if he so much as moved.[25]

The two men are not paragons of beauty! Grave Digger Jones looks like any seasoned Harlem tough, while Coffin Ed Johnson, his face disfigured by an acid-throwing gangster and patched up with skin tissue from his thigh that has subsequently turned a lighter shade, resembles a Black Dracula, a Harlem Frankenstein. But then their theatre of operations is not an average police precinct:

Looking eastward from the towers of Riverside Church, perched among the university buildings on the high banks of the Hudson River, in a valley far below, waves of gray rooftops distort the perspective like the surface of a sea. Below the surface, in the murky waters of fetid tenements, a city of black people who are convulsed in desperate living, like the voracious churning of millions of hungry cannibal fish. Blind mouths eating their own guts. Stick in a hand and draw back a nub. That is Harlem.[26]

One of its most depraved streets has been baptized the Bucket-of-Blood by the underworld. A haunt of heistmen and muggers. Enter one of its tenement buildings and you will find Dante's *Inferno* rewritten by an underground magazine:

Graffiti decorated the whitewashed walls. Huge genitals hung from crude dwarfed torsos like a harvest of strange fruit. Someone had drawn a nude couple in a sex embrace. Others had added to it. Now it was a mural.[27]

It is a grotesque, almost unreal world characterized by the names people bear: a shoeshine boy is called Aesop Pickins, a parking-lot attendant Socrates X. Hoover; Ready Belcher is a pimp, Big Smiley a barman, a gang of youthful toughs – Bones, Sheik, Choo-Choo, and Inky – goes by the name of the 'Real Cool Moslems'. Big Smiley wields a sharply honed axe when his customers misbehave, 'skivs' (knifes) and 'heaters' (guns) are freely used; pick-pockets, perverts, prostitutes, and dope-pushers abound. Women are named in the most tantalizing fashion – Lotus Green, Sassafras, Sugartit, and Honey Bee. They never betray you; gentle creatures that they are, they merely 'turn you in for a new model'. For spiritual comfort, Harlemites crowd around preachers like Jesus Baby, or Reverend Converted Sinner, or Sweet Prophet Brown, whose Church of Wonderful Prayer is always open to those who can afford to bring out a wad of greenbacks to pay for the breadcrumbs in his ermine-lined pocket. For the poorest of the poor there is still Sister Gabriel, the austere, Bible-quoting 'sister of mercy' – actually a transvestite drug addict – who sells tickets to heaven inscribed 'Admit one' at a dollar apiece. When all earthly devices fail, even marijuana, which has the marvellous power to change the Bucket-of-Blood into the Heavenly Jerusalem, and Harlemites, always mindful of the fact that 'we all got to go when the wagon comes', prepare to meet their Maker, Mr H. Exodus Clay, the prosperous undertaker, is pleased to oblige. To beat his competitors to it, he will send his sweet chariot to carry you home even before your body gets cold (see *The Big Gold Dream*).

The Harlem novels of Chester Himes are not tortuous whodunits, more or less artificial exercises in abstract logic comprising a fixed number of characters in search of a murderer. In the first place they create an atmosphere and a social climate with a distinctive group expression which is unmistakably that of Harlem, just as Dashiell Hammett conjures up San Francisco, Raymond Chandler Los Angeles, and Georges Simenon Paris, or some small provincial French town. The plot evolving within this setting mostly belongs to what we might call the treasure-hunt variety – a mad rush of several interested parties, working at cross-purposes, from one clue to the next: a modernized form of the picaresque novel. The great hunt often turns out futile in the end; the elusive 'treasure' that always leaves assorted dead bodies in its wake will more likely than not be discovered to be a fake in the classical manner of Hammett's *Maltese Falcon*, or simply non-existent. In *All Shot Up*, the 50,000 dollars' haul of party funds everybody is after has been stolen by the 'victim' even before the 'heist' arranged by him sets the ball rolling. In *Cotton Comes to Harlem* the mysterious bale of cotton that played a role in the raid on the fund-raising Bar-B-Q of the Reverend O'Malley's 'Back to Africa Movement' is finally found to be empty inside. The consignment of heroin in *The Heat's On* that spelt the death of several underworld characters and gave Coffin Ed and Grave Digger their long-awaited chance to pour their .38 slugs into some white professional killers drugged to the gills has been inadvertently burned in the furnace of the central heating before the story opens.

The pattern becomes more intricate in *For Love of Imabelle*. Jackson, the hard-working, church-going assistant of undertaker H. Exodus Clay, is 'played for a sucker' by his woman Imabelle:

> She was a cushioned-lipped, hot-bodied, banana-skin chick with the speckled-brown eyes of a teaser and the high-arched, ball-bearing hips of a natural-born *amante*. Jackson was as crazy about her as moose for doe.[28]

The racketeers with whom Imabelle is associated specialize in two confidence-tricks: firstly 'The Blow' (i.e. 'raising' money – a technique known as 'money-doubling' in West Africa, apparently one of the less respectable cultural survivals indulged in by the black community in the USA); and secondly, the 'lost-gold-mine pitch', or selling shares for a non-existent Mexican gold-mine. Although duped out of all his savings by means of 'The Blow', Jackson never wavers and his faith in his woman remains unshaken. In a nightmarish drive through Harlem in a stolen hearse he tries to save her trunk of solid gold ore, with a reasonable fraction of the New York City Police Force in hot pursuit. What he does not know is that instead of gold ore the trunk contains the body of a dead gangster and that the treasure, when eventually found in a coalbin, turns out to be fool's gold.

The Big Gold Dream reverses the pattern. Here a good-for-nothing, parasitical male, Sugar Stonewall, tries to bamboozle his 'square' lady-friend Alberta Wright ('an upright, God-fearing, Christian woman') but gets caught up in the process by more competent con-men who in their turn are conned in successive stages reminiscent of a Russian doll. The treasure of 100,000 brand-new dollars discovered in Alberta's sofa is nothing more than a red herring, for it happens to consist of Confederate money, and the final trace fatefully leads to the Temple of Wonderful Prayer and the proponent of religious capitalism, Sweet Prophet Brown.

Although Chester Himes's latest novel to date – *Blind Man with a Pistol* – belongs to the revolving stage of the Harlem *Comédie Humaine*, with toughs, freaks, and fairies bestriding the scene, and the two crack detectives, Coffin Ed and Grave Digger, as hard-hitting as ever, it also forms a class all of its own. Its atmosphere is more highly charged, crime and sexuality reach a fever pitch, while the high comedy of the earlier books is reduced to a more sombre mood. The novel attains an eminently political dimension, not through overt preaching but through the introduction of mass scenes involving rival political movements on the one hand, and the changing outlook of the two black detectives on the other. They are becoming more and more disgruntled with the existing order, which for Harlem spells lingering chaos even under the serenest surface. There are now new factors to be reckoned with in the power-game, and on one occasion, when Coffin Ed and Grave Digger need information, they no longer rely on their habitual stool-pigeons but seek the advice of the Black Moslem leader, the Reverend Michael X. Their nerves seem to be always on edge, and they have shed the bonhomie with which they used to treat their superior officer, the white Lieutenant Anderson. There is no more easy solution to clearly defined criminal cases, whether it is the killing of a lonely white pleasure-seeker or a riotous assembly with arson and attempted murder involving thousands of people. The investigation of the former incident bogs down in a blind alley, with clues vanishing and material witnesses dying mysterious deaths. When dealing with the latter, Coffin Ed and Grave Digger, for all their efforts, end up empty-handed. Michael X cryptically speaks of a certain Mr Big but refuses to elucidate. The two detectives finally report to their superior officer that the person responsible for the riot is just as dead as the witnesses in the murder case they have been working on. Hard pressed by Lt Anderson to disclose his identity, they reveal that it is a man called Abraham Lincoln, who freed the negro slaves without making provision to feed them.

The answer here given by Himes is reminiscent of Eldridge Cleaver's verdict in a similar situation described in *Soul on Ice*:

> Old funny-styled, zipper-mouthed political night riders know nothing but to haul out an investigating committee *to look into the disturbance* to

find the cause of the unrest among the youth. Look into a mirror. The cause is you, Mr. and Mrs. Yesterday, you with your forked tongues.[29]

But this surprise solution which defies the rules of the well-made detective novel for the benefit of political allegory is not the last word. Only now is the theme of the novel unleashed, in an epilogue which sheds the flamboyant naturalism of the Harlem series for a spontaneous, horrifying Surrealism. An angered black man, blind as a mole, issues forth from the bowels of the earth – a Harlem subway station – and starts shooting enemy and soul brother alike. Himes here seizes upon an archetypal situation described by the chief ideologist of the Surrealist School thus:

> The simplest surrealist act, writes Breton . . . consists of going down into the street, gun in hand, and shooting into the crowd at random as long as possible.[30]

This epilogue, which signifies *unorganized violence* born of despair, is at the same time the prologue to a different kind of violence advocated by Himes, which dwarfs the proportions of the race war he predicted in an article published in *The Chicago Defender* in 1945 under the title, 'Equality for 125,000 Dead'. In 1969 his estimate had gone up to 3 million dead 'even if most, or at least two-thirds, were Black people themselves'.[31] Paradoxically, the whole sanguinary exercise is not envisaged as a contribution to 'the rotting and destruction of America', as in the apocalyptic visions of LeRoi Jones who wants only the Nation of Islam to survive Armageddon, but as a fountain of youth from which a society of equals will arise. Chester Himes is an integrationist with a vengeance.

During the darkest days of his career as a writer after the débâcle of *Lonely Crusade*, Chester Himes dumbfounded his audience at the University of Chicago in 1948 by defending the Negro's right to hate whites. At the same time, however, he emphasized his American-ness: 'The American Negro, we must remember, is an American; the face may be the face of Africa, but the heart has the beat of Wall Street.'[32]

The lesson of his latest novel having been 'that all unorganized violence is like a blind man with a pistol', the 60-year-old militant in the same year proceeded to draw the visionary portrait of *a seeing man with an automatic rifle* – a paradigm of organized violence – in a short prose sketch, 'Prediction' (1969). From his hideout in the poor box of the big cathedral, symbolically firing through 'the slot in the wall for donations', he checkmates a police parade of 6,000 men marching through the big city like rams to the slaughter:

> He experienced spiritual ecstasy to see the brains flying from those white men's heads, to see the fat arrogant bodies of the whites shattered and broken apart, cast into death. Hate served his pleasure; he thought

fleetingly and pleasurably of all the humiliations and hurts imposed on him and all blacks by whites; in less than a second the complete outrage of slavery flashed across his mind and he could see the whites with a strange, pure clarity eating the flesh of the blacks and he knew at last that they were the only real cannibals who had ever existed . . .[33]

Whatever one considers 'Prediction' to be – a product of fantasy revenge or the 1984 of American race relations, a piece of science fiction or a political manifesto – it powerfully conveys one of the profoundest convictions of Chester B. Himes, writer and prophet:

I believe the Black man in America holds the destiny of the entire Western world.[34]

NOTES

1. 'Chester Himes, Traveler on the Long, Rough, Lonely Old Road', interview by Hoyt W. Fuller, Alicante (Spain), 15 May 1969, in *Black World*, New York, A Johnson Publication, March 1972, p. 6.
2. Chester Himes, *The Quality of Hurt: The Autobiography of Chester Himes*, London, Michael Joseph, 1973, pp. 101–12.
3. *The Quality* . . ., p. 132. (Hereinafter *QH*.)
4. Chester Himes, *The Primitive*, New York, NAL/Signet, 1955, p. 22. (Hereinafter *TP*.)
5. *QH*, p. 48.
6. James Baldwin, 'Alas, Poor Richard', in *Nobody Knows My Name*, London, Transworld Publishers Ltd (Corgi Books), 1965, pp. 166–7. See also Himes's spirited defence of Wright when the latter is criticized *in absentia* by 'an assemblage of Jewish intellectuals from all over Europe', in *QH*, pp. 210–11.
7. Chester Himes, *L'Aveugle au pistolet* (Blind Man with a Pistol), Paris, Gallimard, 1970, preface by Marcel Duhamel, p. 7.
8. 'Amid the Alien Corn', *Time Magazine*, 17 November 1958, p. 28.
9. Jesse shrugged. 'Jesus Christ. It's a good thing he isn't living now. His friends would never get a book published about him.'
    Pope laughed. 'You're a hell of a good writer, Jesse. Why don't you write a Negro success novel? An inspirational story? The public is tired of the poor downtrodden Negro.' (*The Primitive*, p. 94.)
10. Chester Himes. 'Four Essays Written During the Second World War', in *Black on Black*, New York, Doubleday, 1973, pp. 213–35.
11. 'Amid the Alien Corn', loc. cit.
12. Chester Himes, *Lonely Crusade*, London, Falcon Press, 1950, p. 50. (Hereinafter *LC*.)
13. Chester Himes, 'Dilemma of the Negro Novelist in the United States', in *Beyond the Angry Black*, ed. John A. Williams, New York and Toronto, NAL/Signet, 1971, p. 74.

14. Hans Habe, *Der Tod in Texas*, München/Wein/Basel, Verlag Kurt Desch, 1964, pp. 34, 55.
15. John A. Williams, 'My Man Himes – An Interview with Chester Himes', in *Amistad 1*, ed. J. A. Williams and C. F. Harris, New York, Random House/Vintage Books, 1970, p. 31.
16. Chester Himes, *The Third Generation*, New York, NAL/Signet, 1956, p. 37. (Hereinafter *3rd G.*)
17. Blyden Jackson, 'Blithe Newcomers', *Phylon*, XVI, 1955, p. 9.
18. Chester Himes, *If He Hollers Let Him Go*, London, Falcon Press, 1947, p. 153.
19. James Baldwin, 'Everybody's Protest Novel', in *Notes of a Native Son*, Boston, The Beacon Press, 1953, p. 20. See also p. 7.
20. 'Fanon wrote a long article on my "Treatment of Violence" which his wife still has, and which I've thought I might get and have published. Because he had the same feeling, of course, that I have.' John A. Williams, 'My Man Himes . . .', op. cit., p. 87.
21. Eldridge Cleaver in *Soul on Ice*, reprinted in *Alienated Man*, ed. Eva Taube, New Jersey, Hayden Book Company Inc., 1972, p. 138.
22. The term is used by the blithe latecomer, Blyden Jackson, in *Black Poetry in America*, Baton Rouge, Louisiana State University Press, 1974, p. 89 (co-authored with Louis D. Rubin, Jr).
23. 'I started to write the definitive book on the Black Revolution . . . I have always believed . . . that the Black man in America should mount a serious revolution and this revolution should employ a massive, extreme violence.' Chester Himes when interviewed by Hoyt W. Fuller, 1969, op. cit., p. 18.
24. 'Shooting people in the head generates power. This is what I think black writers should write about. I remember Sartre made a statement which was recorded in the French press (I never had any use for Sartre since) that in writing his play *The Respectful Prostitute* he recognized the fact that a black man could not assault a white person in America. *That's one of the reasons I began writing the detective story. I wanted to introduce the idea of violence.* [My italics.] After all, Americans live by violence, and violence achieves – regardless of what any one says, regardless of the distaste of the white community – its own ends.' John A. Williams, 'My Man Himes . . .', op. cit., p. 75.
25. Chester Himes, *All Shot Up*, New Jersey, The Chatham Bookseller, 1973, p. 30.
26. Chester Himes, *For Love of Imabelle*, New Jersey, The Chatham Bookseller, 1973, p. 111.
27. ibid., p. 113.
28. ibid., p. 6.
29. Eldridge Cleaver in *Soul on Ice*, reprinted in *Black Viewpoints*, ed. Arthur C. Littleton and Mary W. Burger, New York, NAL/Signet, 1971, p. 255.
30. Jean-Paul Sartre, 'Qu'est-ce que la littérature', *Situations*, II, Paris, Gallimard, 1948, p. 172 (my translation).
31. Interview by Hoyt W. Fuller, loc. cit.
32. Chester Himes, 'Dilemma of the Negro Novelist . . .', op cit., p. 77. Cf. also: 'To hate white people is one of the first emotions an American

Negro develops when he becomes old enough to learn what his status is in American society. He must, of necessity, hate white people. He would not be ... human if he did not develop a hatred for his oppressors', op. cit., p. 78.

33. Chester Himes, 'Prediction' in *Black on Black* ('Baby Sister' and selected writings), New York, Doubleday, 1973, p. 286.
34. Interview by Hoyt W. Fuller, loc. cit.

BOOKS BY CHESTER HIMES IN CHRONOLOGICAL ORDER

French translations are only listed for the Harlem series.
AT = alternative title.
HS = Harlem series.

1. *If He Hollers Let Him Go*, New York, Doubleday, Doran & Co, 1945. Reprinted by New American Library (NAL), 1950. Reprinted by Berkley Publishing Corporation, (Berkley Books) New York, 1955. Reprinted by NAL/Signet, New York, 1971. Reprinted by Falcon Press, London, 1947. Reprinted by Sphere Books, London, 1967.
2. *Lonely Crusade*, New York, Alfred A. Knopf, 1947. Reprinted by World Publishing Company, Cleveland, Ohio, 1948. Reprinted by Falcon Press, London, 1950.
3. *Cast the First Stone*, New York, Coward-McCann, 1952. Reprinted by NAL/Signet, New York, 1972.
4. *The Third Generation*, New York, World Publishing Company, 1954. Reprinted by NAL/Signet, New York, 1956. Reissued by The Chatham Bookseller, Chatham, NJ, 1975.
5. *The Primitive*, New York, NAL/Signet, 1955.
6. (HS) *For Love of Imabelle*, Greenwich, Conn., Fawcett Publication, 1957.
   La Reine des pommes, Paris, Gallimard, Série Noire, 1958.
   (AT) American edition slightly revised as *The Five-Cornered Square*, New York, Hearst Corporation, An Avon Original, 1964.
   (AT) *A Rage in Harlem*, London, Panther Books, 1969. Reprinted as *For Love of Imabelle* by the Dell Publishing Company, New York, 1971, and reissued under the same title by The Chatham Bookseller, Chatham, NJ, 1973.
7. (HS) *Il Pleut des coups durs*, Paris, Gallimard, SN, 1958, 1967.
   The Real Cool Killers, New York, Avon Publications, 1959. Reprinted as a Berkley Medallion Book, New York, 1966. Reprinted by Panther Books, London, 1969.
   (AT) Original title: *If Trouble was Money*.
8. (HS) *Couché dans le pain*, Paris, Gallimard, SN, 1959.
   The Crazy Kill, New York, Hearst Corporation, An Avon Original, 1959. Reprinted by Panther Books, London, 1968.
   (AT) Original title: *A Jealous Man Can't Win*.
9. (HS) *Dare-dare*, Paris, Gallimard, SN, 1959.

Run, Man, Run, New York, Putnam's Sons, 1966. Reprinted by F. Muller, London, 1967. Reprinted as a Dell paperback by the Dell Publishing Corporation, New York, 1969.

NB This is the only volume in the Harlem series without the characters of Coffin Ed Johnson and Grave Digger Jones (ed. Cercueil et Fossoyeur).

10. (HS) *Tout pour plaire*, Paris, Gallimard, SN, 1959.
The Big Gold Dream, New York, Hearst Corporation, An Avon Original, 1960. Reprinted as a Berkley Paperback by Berkley Publishing Corporation, New York, 1966. Reissued by The Chatham Bookseller, Chatham, NJ, 1973.

11. (HS) *Imbroglio Negro*, Paris, Gallimard, SN, 1960, 1968.
All Shot Up, New York, Hearst Corporation, An Avon Original, 1960. Reprinted as a Berkley Paperback, 1966. Reprinted by Panther Books, London, 1968. Reissued by The Chatham Bookseller, Chatham, NJ, 1973.
(AT) Original title: *Don't Play with Death*.

12. (HS) *Ne nous énervons pas*, Paris, Gallimard, SN, 1961.
The Heat's On, New York, Putnam's Sons, 1966. Reprinted by F. Muller, London, 1966. Reprinted by Dell Publishing Corporation New York, 1967, 1968.
(AT) Original title: *Be Calm*.

13. *Pinktoes*, Paris, Olympia Press, 1961.
Mamie Mason, ou, Un exercice de la bonne volonté, Paris, Plon, 1962. Revised American edition of *Pinktoes* by Dell & Putnam, New York, 1967, 1969. English edition by Arthur Baker, London, 1965. Reprinted by Transworld Publishers/Corgi Books, London, 1967.
(AT) Original title: *Mamie Mason*.

14. (HS) *Retour en Afrique, ou, Le Casse de l'oncle Tom*, Paris, Plon, 1963.
Cotton Comes to Harlem, New York, Putnam's Sons, 1963. Reprinted in paperback by the Dell Publishing Corporation, New York, 1966, 1970. Reprinted by Panther Books, London, 1969.

15. *Une Affaire de viol* (= A Case of Rape, published in French only). Paris, Editions Les Yeux ouverts, 1963.

16. (HS) *Blind Man with a Pistol*, New York, William Morrow, 1969.
(AT) Reprinted in paperback as *Hot Day, Hot Night* by the Dell Publishing Corporation, New York, 1970. *L'Aveugle au pistolet*, Paris, Gallimard, Collection 'Du Monde Entier', 1970.

17. *The Quality of Hurt*. The Autobiography of Chester Himes, Vol I, New York, Doubleday, 1972.
English edition: London, Michael Joseph, 1973.

18. *Black on Black* ('Baby Sister' and selected writings), New York, Doubleday, 1973.

The Peasant Novel in Haiti

J. M. Dash

One of the more misleading notions inherited from the ideology of Negritude has been the tendency to consider all black writing as constituting one homogeneous and uniform literary bloc. Since the orthodox Negritude position was that the colonial past was nothing but a catalogue of shame and injustice, the only alternative for these victims of history who made up the black diaspora was a close identification with a monolithic pan-African ideal. This ideological position seemed politically valid and strategic in the 1950s with the emergence of numerous Third World states which shared the common past of colonialism and were then seeking political autonomy. Negritude clearly responded to the desperate desire to be free of the colonial past and also provided a much-needed feeling of solidarity. However, what was a necessary political manoeuvre in the 1950s can now be seen to involve some measure of simplification as to the process of cultural evolution. What had not been taken into account was the possibility that in spite of the unjust nature of the colonial system, various communities might have evolved certain characteristics that had transformed them into distinct national communities. Consequently the concept of an international neo-African culture could only serve in the long run to obscure this important diversity. Indeed it was slowly becoming apparent that Negritude could become an ideology which demanded a literary conformity which was artistically debilitating and could lead to an uncreative literary preciosity among black writers. Wole Soyinka's statement that a tiger does not proclaim his tigritude was made in response to this tendency.

The literature that perhaps has suffered the most from the application of this universalizing myth is that of Haiti. Haiti, independent since 1804, presents a special and unparalleled historical and cultural situation. For instance literary tendencies apparent in other Third World countries in the last few decades were already part of the Haitian literary tradition in the nineteenth century. Conclusive proof of Haiti's uniqueness in this respect can be seen in the evolution of the novel form. This genre which appears as a relatively recent literary phenomenon in French West African writing – for instance Camara Laye's *L'Enfant Noir* only appeared in 1954 – has existed in Haiti since the late nineteenth century. The unique evolution of this genre in Haiti is apparent in the fact that from its earliest manifestation the Haitian novel has gone beyond anti-colonial polemics, beyond recording the *Angst* of the *assimilé*, to analysing the experience of survival of the Haitian people, particularly the peasantry, in a specific post-colonial and national context. The source of inspiration for this genre was found in the reality of the peasant community whose very existence attested to the creation of a distinct and independent cultural entity. In the cultural 'marronage' of the folk – their capacity for adapting their consciousness to the historical imperatives of the New World, indeed to circumvent the tragic ironies of the colonial and post-independence experience – the Haitian writer found a rich body of material that for almost a century has supported a very special tradition in Haitian literature: the Peasant Novel.

THE NINETEENTH CENTURY AND THE HAITIAN NOVEL

Probably the most important influence on Haitian literature in the nineteenth century was the Romantic movement. It signified the possibility of breaking away from the confining poetics of classicism and, with its emphasis on national literatures and the diversity and freedom of literary expression, it did much to liberate the creative imagination of Haitian writers. It is in the mid-nineteenth century that one can situate the beginning of a preoccupation with 'La Muse Haitienne' in Haitian writing. The Haitian novel which did not emerge until very late in the nineteenth century inherited this literary nationalism.

This is not to say that such literary nationalism was widespread and acceptable to all Haitian writers. A commentator on Haitian writing in the nineteenth century produced, in a series of articles entitled 'Les Deux Tendances' (The Two Tendencies), flexible criteria for evaluating what he considered a cosmopolitan and an indigenous trend among Haitian writers:

> ... it seems to me that we have not only one but two literatures; one which is closely linked to our national history, from which it draws its inspiration, which is purely Haitian; the other which is attracted to depicting the whole human condition, which contains a wider, more universal appeal, which we shall term franco or humano Haitian.[1]

The universal trend in Haitian writing was linked closely to the Symbolist insistence on aestheticism and an anti-materialist approach to literary creativity. The Indigenist position could be similarly linked to the ideology and conventions of the Realist and Naturalist movements in

France. This second tendency was responsible for that strong, regionalist quality in Haitian novels at the time.

The Haitian novelist of the late nineteenth century had borrowed from his metropolitan contemporaries a conception of the novel as a record (more precisely a mirror) of external socio-historical reality. The novel was to be a kind of sociological investigation of society which would eventually reveal universal truths of the human condition. Man was not an abstraction but a particular individual whose existence was determined by his environment. What Zola had done for the urban poor in France, the Haitians wished to do for their own society. One of the most vocal Haitian novelists of the time, Frederic Marcelin, defended the creative potential of the national experience: '. . . our literature must find a greater source of inspiration in our history, our material and moral topography, in all the physical beauty of our country. Their praises must be sung for them to be loved.'[2]

Along with the legacy of photographic realism came the element of social consciousness particularly apparent in those who portrayed the peasantry in their work. Zola's social commitment to the oppressed in France created among Haitian artists an equal sympathy for the Haitian peasant. What was desired was more than local colour and sensationalism. There is evidence of a strong, emotional commitment to exposing the harsh realities of peasant life:

> Think a little of these wretched, rural folk, common fodder for our appetites, for our passions, unwitting tools, playthings in our quarrels. We have devastated, ruined their fields, we have pitilessly dismembered, dislocated their humble families, we have in the end sent them to their deaths.[3]

The mimetic value of the novel form and a strong social conscience seem fundamental to the creative imagination of the nineteenth-century Haitian novelist. There now emerge two important themes in these works of the turn of the century – political satire and the depiction of the peasantry. As far as the former is concerned, novels published at the turn of the century contained numerous parodies, in the manner of Flaubert, of the pretentions of the corrupt political demagogue. Frederic Marcelin's *Themistocle Epaminondas Labasterre* (1901) is a very good example of this kind of political satire.

What is more important for our purposes is the literary experimentation involved in realizing the second area of interest at the time – the peasantry. Justin L'herisson's *La Famille des Pitite Caille* (1905) is an interesting attempt at creating real originality in the novel form. Using a narrative framework drawn from the Haitian oral tradition, L'herisson dramatically describes the adventures of his naive 'nouveau riche' protagonist in a mixture of the vernacular and standard French. Semi-literate and of peasant origins, Eliezer Pitite Caille's pretensions are mercilessly satirized by the revelation of his shallowness and ignorance. Already we have in this short but effective work the literary experimentation with the realities of rural Haiti – even if for the purpose of satire.

In another attempt at literary originality, Antoine Innocent's *Mimola* (1906) descends directly into the peasant experience. In this novel which deals with the use of the Vaudou religion by Madame Georges to cure her daughter Mimola, we have descriptions of the peasant milieu and rituals so detailed they verge on the ethnographic. The value of this work does not lie in its qualities as a novel – since plot and characterization seem contrived and improbable – but in the author's sensitivity to the need for recording the various customs and traditions of the peasant experience.

Even though at the turn of the century this interest in the Haitian peasant produced interesting literary experiments, it created no real masterpiece. But this literary avant-garde is important as the beginning of a tradition in the Haitian novel that would later produce the persuasive and sophisticated novels of the post-Occupation period.

THE OCCUPATION AND JACQUES ROUMAIN

The American Occupation of Haiti (1915–34) represents an important turning point in that country's political and literary consciousness. The ambivalence that existed among some intellectuals as far as the indigenous culture was concerned was now replaced by a militant nationalism in the face of the American presence. It was the aim of the post-Occupation generation to make admissible in art a reality whose worthiness was once questioned by some. It is this unity of intention that distinguishes this generation and later results in novels that bring artistic credibility and a genuine emotional resonance to the experience of Haiti's peasantry.

Concern for Haiti's peasants and interest in the peasant novel are revived during the Occupation period because of the short-lived peasant revolt against the Americans. Indeed Charlemagne Péralte and his band of irregulars – called 'cacos' and drawn from peasant communities – were the only ones to offer armed resistance to the American marines. This uprising was brutally put down and thousands of peasants were killed. With the increase of nationalist sentiments the peasant struggle began to be considered a heroic symbol in the attempt to regain national sovereignty. Political and subsequent literary interest became an integral part of anti-American polemics.

Literary investigation of peasant culture in the 1930s was greatly facilitated by the work of Jean Price-Mars, whose documentary work on peasant culture, *Ainsi Parla l'Oncle*, published in 1928, criticized the prejudices and ambivalence of the traditional elite and encouraged interest in the peasant experience. His attack was directed against 'le bovarysme collectif' – the collective cultural ambivalence – of the traditional intellectual. Through ethnographic studies, he attempted to legitimize the study of peasant culture and remove the stigma attached to the African past. His exhortations had an enormous impact on writers in the 1930s:

> The subject of our literature should sometimes be drawn from the immense reserve which is our folklore, in which the motives for our volition have been condensed for centuries, in which the elements of our sensibility have been developed, in which our character as a people has been moulded, that is our national soul.[4]

This refusal to see the national experience and the African heritage as hopeless and confining was a timely and necessary undertaking. It responded directly to the crisis of identity and the need for cultural authenticity posed by the Occupation.

Price-Mars's exhortations and the political imperatives of the times created in the late 1920s the literary movement of Indigenism. *La Revue Indigéne* founded in 1927 was meant to serve as a defence and illustration of *l'âme haitienne*. Literary activity in this period is centred on poetry and it is not until the 1930s that the tradition of the peasant novel is revived in the context of the polemics of the Occupation period.

To illustrate the new directions taken by Haiti's novelists we will concentrate on two of the more important writers who attempted to deal with the peasant experience in fiction – Jacques Roumain and Philippe Thoby Marcelin. The latter, with an established reputation as an indigenist poet, tended to reveal in his fiction a strong regionalist tendency and at times a disappointing penchant for the sensational and the exotic. In these novels, *Canapé Vert* (1944), *La Bête de Museau* (1946), and *Le Crayon de Dieu* (1951), the reader is plunged into a world of mystery and the supernatural. However, beyond the anthropological interest that such a world creates, the novels fail to convince us of the humanity of the protagonists involved. Perhaps Marcelin was so influenced by *The Magic Island* of William Seabrook[5] that his own novels could be no more than sensational and bizarre. Fanon's description of the depiction of the peasantry by 'the native intellectual' seems particularly applicable here: 'The culture that the intellectual leans towards is often no more than a stock of particularisms. He wishes to attach himself to the people; but instead he only catches hold of their outer garments.'[6]

In contrast, Roumain's contribution to the peasant novel showed a real attempt at closely defining the nature of the genre, eventually providing new literary possibilities for it. Price-Mars's encouragement of the investigation of peasant culture as a means of determining *l'âme nationale* contained one important drawback. It tended to obscure and gloss over the grim reality of the Haitian peasant community. Indeed, as far as the Vaudou religion is concerned, he underestimated the tragic potential of an excessive dependence on the supernatural. Rémy Bastien, in a later assessment of Price-Mars's theories, remarks:

> There is no way of determining whether or not his intention was to make the peasant and his culture acceptable to the city elite, but the ethnography of Price-Mars' book is one-sided, prudently ignoring the disastrous power of magic, the precarious economy and the diseases in Haitian communities.[7]

Those who, like Marcelin, followed Price-Mars's theories unquestioningly failed to present objectively the full nature of the experience but instead, as in Marcelin's case, reveal a gratuitous catalogue of fantasy and melodrama in their work.

As we have seen before, the peasant novel at the turn of the century demanded not only objectivity but the necessity of a social conscience. Jacques Roumain's fiction in the 1930s revived this important element in the peasant novel. His early novels in the 1930s treated both sides of Haitian society – the urban bourgeoisie and the peasantry – and came to the same conclusion. In the collections of short stories *La Proie et L'Ombre* (1930) and *Les Fantoches* (1931) we have a penetrating insight into the impotence and sterility of the urban elite. The older generation is, as a parasitic elite, trapped in the prejudices of culture and class, and the younger generation cannot break free from this confinement. His depiction of the Haitian peasantry is no different. In the early short novel *La Montagne Ensorcelée* (1931), Roumain penetrates beyond the fantastic and supernatural to present a chilling vision of ritual murder in a peasant community.

This early work is not preoccupied with celebrating the cultural uniqueness of the Haitian people but presents a moving picture of the way in which superstition and ignorance can be responsible for irrational and inhuman acts. It is a demonstration of the way in which peasant religion had become a form of spiritual refuge for the fears and chronic insecurity of the peasantry. In this work a small peasant community, stricken by poverty, is suffering from an interminable drought and their only explanation is that they have been cursed by their gods. As the story progresses, a series of other misfortunes occurs and an old woman who lives apart from the rest of the villagers is suspected of witchcraft. In order to rid themselves of their misery, the villagers resort to a ritual murder. The old woman is stoned and beaten to death by a mob:

She stumbled, wavered for a second, then fell. A wave of screams crashed over her, blows fell, she did not utter a cry, but her bones cracked under the blows like dry wood. It did not stop until she was little more than a small soft bag of mud and blood.[8]

They then complete their vengeance by beheading the daughter:

The flash slashes down with a whistle, the head severed rolls a bit on the grass.
Everyone flees, except Balletray who stares, his eyes empty, at the matchette, the body, the body, the machette. (pp. 187-8)

The ideological and aesthetic distance between Marcelin and Roumain is evident. Roumain's tale reaches beyond melodrama and ethnology to present the tragic human truth of primitive stagnation. In this respect there is an interesting parallel between Roumain's depiction of the peasantry and Sembène Ousmane's main character in *Le Mandat*. Dieng's submissiveness reveals Ousmane's view of the limitations of the peasant culture in its inability to provide a solution as well as the author's refusal to glorify blindly the culture of the folk.

In order to explain the economic exploitation and spiritual impotence observed in Haitian society, Roumain turned to Marxism. What is interesting in Roumain's Marxism is his adaptation of this ideology to the specifics of the Haitian situation. For instance, on the subject of peasant culture Roumain was violently against the persecution of those who practised the Vaudou religion and saw the importance of documenting the rituals and customs involved. Yet he could also see the limitations of this culture and saw the necessity of bringing enlightenment to peasant communities:

If we wish to change the archaic religious mentality of our peasants, they must be educated. And they cannot be educated unless we transform at the same time the material conditions in which they live . . . As long as there is no competent system of rural clinics, the peasant will consult his 'bocor' [priest]. And he is right in doing so.[9]

Roumain's *Gouverneurs de la rosée* (Masters of the dew), published posthumously in 1944, attempted to combine the author's Marxism with his vision of the peasant experience – that is, to provide a solution for the pessimism of his early work. To this extent his last novel can be considered a *roman à thèse*. He does not only present peasant reality but projects his own ideological vision on to it. This represented an entirely new departure for the peasant novel and Roumain set himself the difficult objective of including political ideology in the novel form. It is in this respect that Roumain's achievement is significant because in *Gouverneurs de la rosée* we are emotionally moved before we are intellectually persuaded. Indeed, the

Marxist element in this novel is not merely an illustration of party dogma but seems to stem from the larger human and moral vision that such an ideology provides. The plot concerns Manuel's return to the peasant community of Fonds-Rouge, after working in Cuba. He finds the village stricken by a drought and divided by an intense family feud. He attacks the resignation endemic in his village by preaching the gospel of political awareness and illustrates his ideas in a tangible way by bringing water to Fonds-Rouge through the collective labour of the villagers. Even though he is killed in attempting to reconcile the two warring factions in the novel, the villagers have learnt to transform their environment and become 'masters of the dew'. The political nature of the plot is obvious but Roumain is careful in this political fable to create an authentic and convincing humanity in his main character. As a result, a similar political novel such as Zobel's *Diab'la* (1947) seems clumsy and contrived, because sufficient care is not taken to graft the political message on to a credible situation.

Roumain makes no excessive demands on our credulity, as details such as Manuel's acquisition of the Marxist creed are explained by his stay in Cuba. If he had never left he would be resigned like the others in Fonds-Rouge. He is also rooted in his community and landscape and by no means the didactic, idealized 'porte-parole' of the author. Manuel's intimate relationship with the land is always apparent. The magical, pantheistic experience is carefully recorded by Roumain.

> He felt like singing a salutation to the trees: Plants o my plants, I tell you! 'honour'; you will reply: 'respect', so that I can enter. You are my home, you are my country. Plants, I say: lianas of my forest, I too have been planted in this earth.[10]

Another interesting and revealing incident which again makes Manuel into less of an ideological abstraction is the fact that his newly acquired enlightenment has not completely obliterated the past. In spite of his awareness of the limitations of peasant religion he can not resist the overpowering effect of the Vaudou ritual:

> Manuel, overcome by the pulsating magic of the drums in the innermost regions of his blood, was dancing and singing with the others. (p. 60)

This important tension between the residue of the past and Manuel's present awareness, the traditional and the progressive, only serves to make him more plausible and convincing within the peasant situation.

In this question of literary authenticity, Roumain's ability to create a strong sense of realism in the novel is directly related to his linguistic achievement. Other attempts to evoke a genuine impression of a peasant community have revolved around using varying degrees of ethnographic detail as to customs, rituals, etc. Roumain's attempts in this novel reproduce the mind of the peasant by creating a French based on the structures of Haitian creole. (The only other comparable attempt to do this is L'hérisson's modest vignette *La Famille des Pitite Caille*.) Not only does Roumain use the actual vocabulary of creole and the proverbs of the peasantry, but he attempts the more complex task of creating a French, comprehensible to a wide audience, which has the sound and texture of creole. For instance expressions such as 'C'est icitte que je reste' and 'Comment va la vie? Je me demande de quel côté est Manuel.' These intrusions of creole emphasize the fact that we are not dealing with political abstraction but with an artistic presentation of peasant reality which has an intense grasp on our imagination.

It is on to this that Roumain's Marxism is grafted. Peasant religion is shown to be a powerful yet desperate retreat for the villagers of Fonds-Rouge:

> ... the ceremony continued. The inhabitants forgot their misery: the dancing and alcohol worked like an anaesthetic, dragging along and drowning their wrecked consciousness in these unreal and forbidding regions where the savage frenzy of their African gods awaited them. (p. 65)

Manuel is painfully aware that this can only be an artificial paradise, that such a ceremony could do little to relieve this condition:

> – No. I have respect for our traditional customs but the blood of a cock or a goat cannot change the seasons, change the direction of the clouds and swell them with water like bladders. (p. 82)

Throughout the novel Manuel is consistent in his appeal to the peasants to learn to control their environment. In this respect traditional customs like the 'coumbite' (a system of collective farming) are used by Manuel to show Fonds-Rouge that unity represents strength and that the essence of this peasant tradition is collective revolt.

Furthermore, what we see in Roumain is not the regionalism and careful anthropology of his predecessors but the peasant novel acquiring a universal kind of significance. The whole of *Gouverneurs de la rosée* is conceived in the universal symbolic terms of decay and renascence as Manuel for instance brings water to the dust and dryness of his village and in spite of his death his message will continue, for his wife is pregnant at the end of the novel. It is the sensitive manipulation of the realist as well as the symbolic qualities in Roumain's novel that bring emotional authority to his depiction of the peasant experience and signify such an important development in the tradition of the peasant novel.

JACQUES STEPHEN ALEXIS

Roumain's contribution to the peasant novel left an enormous literary legacy for those who followed. Jacques Stephen Alexis, who belonged to the generation that succeeded Roumain, reveals in his novels the obvious influence of Roumain's ideas. A Marxist like Roumain, his view of peasant culture and the necessity for an ideological interpretation of the peasant novel is similar to that of his predecessor. Alexis's first novel *Compère Général Soleil* presents us with a main character who feels the same complex relationship to tradition as Manuel did:

> A long time ago the scars and cares of life in town had destroyed in Hilerion his fervent faith in the Vaudou gods . . . the power of a culture as old as the world had lost its hold over him. But suddenly in the heat of this room, all the phantoms of his youth had returned to crowd in on him. He was consumed by them as if by a quivering flame.[11]

Yet as in Roumain there is no gratuitous evocation of folk culture to present the fantastic and bizarre. Alexis also sees the potential limitation of traditional religion. As one character says in Alexis's second novel *Les Arbres Musiciens*:

> The 'loas' [gods] exist in our land because our land is miserable, because you only have your hands and poor primitive tools to cultivate the ground . . . The 'loas' will only die when electricity is brought to the countryside, when light chases the darkness from the huts, when agricultural machines hum in the fields, when the people learn to read and write – when life changes, not before . . .[12]

This obvious Marxist bias clearly situates Alexis as a writer deeply influenced by Roumain's attitude to peasant culture. Yet, realizing the versatility of the literary form he inherited, Alexis sought a further definition of the peasant novel. His comment on Roumain's novel is useful in indicating this new literary orientation:

> The fathers of the Haitian novel, Marcelin, Hibbert, L'hérisson, have left us by their example a formula for narrative technique that does not seem to have attracted Roumain's attention; that of a subtle, detailed, merciless and biting description of Haitian customs . . . that is, a critical realism. In Roumain we find a kind of symbolic realism. The novel attains the form of a great popular poem with classical contours and characters that are pseudo-symbolic.[13]

The important distinction made between Roumain's 'utopian' realism and the tradition of 'critical' realism in the novel is central to Alexis's own definition of the peasant novel. He felt that the fictional form of Roumain, which depended on a powerful interplay of universal symbols and observed reality, suffered the disadvantages of being too far removed from historical reality. Alexis felt the need to dramatize various episodes of Haitian history in his work, thus avoiding the more universal poetic qualities in Roumain's work.

In explaining his position on history and the peasant novel, Alexis noted in 1955:

We must record objectively in our work the things that have happened and are happening now. We must celebrate the experience of our peasants not in an abstract way, undetermined in space and time . . . we must honour the aspirations which occur each morning in every corner of this country, all the emotions of the Haitian people.[14]

Consequently both *Compère Général Soleil* (1955) and *Les Arbres Musiciens* (1957) are situated at very specific times in Haiti's history. The former records the 1934 massacre of Haitian peasants in the Dominican Republic by Trujillo's soldiers. The latter dramatizes the events that took place between 1941 and 1942, during which President Lescot simultaneously gave an American company the right to plant rubber trees on land expropriated from the peasantry and permitted the Catholic Church in Haiti to pursue a campaign against those who practised the Vaudou religion. The religious campaign was being used to serve the economic venture by attempting to destroy the centres of peasant resistance. In attempting to document these specific events in the history of the peasantry, Alexis's novels do not make an ideological departure from those of Roumain, but rather, a literary one.

What Alexis manages to do in his novels is to dramatize the interaction between the individual consciousness and objective historical reality. His main characters reveal this collision of the subjective consciousness and the blind forces of history. As he claimed in 'Où va le roman': 'The classic contradiction in the West between objective reality and inner subjective reality in the novel seems unfounded to me.'[15] This exploration of the individual consciousness is an essential feature of Alexis's novels. He thereby seems to be fulfilling what Lukacs saw as a fundamental condition for the historical novel: 'What matters therefore in the historical novel is not the retelling of great historical events, but the poetic awakening of the people who figured in those events.'[16] It was through his conviction that man's subjectivity transforms and shapes the outer objective reality that Alexis was able to elaborate a very unique perception of history in his work.

At the first conference of black writers in 1956, Alexis raised an important point. The transplanted cultures of the new world had undergone some fundamental changes which he had situated in his characters' perception of historical reality in his novels:

. . . all these glosses and all this gloating over an alleged 'negro-ness' are dangerous in this sense, that they conceal the reality of the cultural autonomy of the Haitian people.[17]

This vision of an independent cultural identity originated in Alexis's own view of the individual's pattern of survival and the way in which his consciousness had been irrevocably and radically transformed in the face of Haiti's history. The conception of a positive historical continuum in Haiti and the New World is based on Alexis's speculation as to an essential interaction of autochthonous, enslaved, and indentured people and the important civilizing legacy they left behind.

The peasantry is not merely manipulated by the rhetoric of protest against historical injustice. To Alexis their survival also indicates an important legacy for the New World. This observation is first apparent in *Les Arbres Musiciens* in which the character of Gonaïbo occurs. Through him Alexis investigates the native consciousness to convey the quality of his response to the violations of colonial history and the ravages of Haiti's politicians. Gonaïbo symbolizes the crucial link with the whole of Haiti's history from pre-Columbian times:

> He was the last son of the red earth of the kingdom of the Golden Flower, he had become the land itself, he thought. He had revived the life of the land as it was in the past. He had the tastes, the colour, the face, the hair of the ancient men of Xaragua. Perhaps by some unsuspected transference of blood their genes had been transmitted to him? (p. 85)

He does not emerge as a casualty of the past but represents a vision of historical continuity, embodying a cosmopolitan memory which provides an entirely new perception of the historical forces that have forged a distinct consciousness in the New World psyche. In Gonaïbo we have a symbol of that continuous process of synthesis which has combined the accretions of previous cultures and the residue of earlier confrontations to directly challenge the myth of 'historylessness'.

In Alexis's last work, this exploration of the peasant consciousness moves into the realm of myths and legend in order to substantiate that inner recreative response to objective reality that we have already seen. *Romancero aux étoiles* (1960) is a collection of stories based on folk tales and myths which have been revitalized and charged with a new contemporary significance. These legends are treated by Alexis as an important medium for presenting the experience of the folk and their imaginative reconstruction of reality. The most complete and original story in this collection is '*Le Sous-Lieutenant Enchanté*' (The Enchanted Sub-Lieutenant). Here we have a highly conscious use of folk legend by Alexis. In this story he creates a symbolic representation of the history of the New World – the quest for material wealth.

This materialistic quest which suggests the various imperialist adventures in the New World is represented by an American soldier's search for gold in

the interior of Haiti. Lt Wheelbarrow epitomizes the archetypal colonizer/
invader with his own materialistic designs in the Caribbean. In the Haitian
interior, the lieutenant is confronted by a totally alien, incomprehensible
world. His initial reaction is to deal with this world in his own terms – to
use his money to establish his authority among the peasants. Yet the
American finds himself immersed in a mythical world that leaves him
totally disoriented. He is continually haunted by a female figure who
symbolizes this world of myth and fantasy:

> She stood upright like an antique statue from the past, sacred, with a
> halo, in her full beauty . . .[18]

Slowly the distinction between the American and this strange world is
blurred and he begins to experience a state of renewal and fulfilment in this
primeval world. The tension between victor and victim becomes irrelevant
as he succumbs to a pervasive sense of harmony with the spiritual. He
records in his diary:

> We had penetrated deep into the heartland for an hour. Arriving at a
> point where it widened out, we stopped and waited in a winding passage.
> There was a certain sweet, pervasive warmth. Against my flesh I could
> feel the vibrations of life radiating from these recesses and the quiver
> of the great thermal currents which dance beneath the sensual earth.
> (p. 209)

From a clash of cultures something new emerges and this legend clearly
indicates the fusion of cultures possible in the imagination of the folk. The
American, his inhibiting materialism undermined, has been shown a whole
new perception of the world. At the end of the tale the lieutenant loses his
life when reality inexorably intrudes. He is accused by the Americans who
invade Haiti in 1915 of consorting with the enemy and is shot, tied up with
his female figure – his newly acquired vision:

> Several old peasants have told me that they saw the lieutenant tied
> together with his companion, and that they were judged and summarily
> executed, accused ·of high treason and consorting with the enemy.
> (p. 212)

Alexis, before his tragic death in 1961, was tentatively elaborating a
reinterpretation of the absurd cycle of Caribbean history through the
legends of the folk. In this unprecedented use of folk material we find the
beginnings of a conception of New World history which, beyond Marxism,
beyond ideology, could be envisaged through the literary imagination. The
creative imagination of black writers has always been involved in a fundamental coming to terms with the past. Through the myths – the imaginative
reconstructing of history – of the folk, Alexis could sense a positive response
to the violations of the past.

It has been suggested that with the disappearance of the colonist the main source of material for black writing has dried up. This may be true of some situations, for instance in the French African novel, where there was once a surge of creativity surrounding the acquisition of independence. The *raison d'être* of this creativity was protest against the colonial presence. Yet this argument can be countered by the evidence in some new literatures of a vital, longstanding literary tradition which does not depend on anticolonial polemics for its survival. The Haitian peasant novel is one such example. And now, at a time when the anti-colonial theme has been exhausted in other literatures, such a tradition can provide fresh literary possibilities which can further substantiate the versatility of the literary imagination.

NOTES

1. *La Jeune Haiti*, February 1896.
2. *Autour de deux romans*, Paris, Imp. Kugelman, 1903, p. 120.
3. ibid., p. 25.
4. *Ainsi Parlal' Oncle*, New York, Parapsychology Foundation, Inc., 1954, p. 192.
5. Cannibalism, the supernatural, atavistic impulses – the primitivist stereotype conveyed by Seabrock – had much to do with justifying the 'civilizing' intention behind the Occupation in the consciences of the American people.
6. *The Wretched of the Earth*, Harmondsworth, Penguin, 1969, p. 180.
7. Rémy Bastien, 'The Role of the Intellectual in a Haitian Plural Society', *Annals of the New York Academy of Sciences*, LXXXIII, January 1960, p. 845.
8. *La Montagne Ensorcelée*, Paris, Editeurs Français Réunis, 1972, p. 180.
9. *A propos de la campagne anti-superstitieuse*, Port-au-Prince, Imp. de L'Etat, p. 12.
10. *Gouverneurs de la rosée*, Paris, Editeurs Français Réunis, 1946, p. 47. (Translation available as *Masters of the Dew*, Caribbean Writers Series, London, Heinemann, 1978 with introduction by Michael Dash.)
11. *Compère Général Soleil*, Paris, Gallimard, 1955, p. 125.
12. *Les Arbres Musiciens*, Paris, Gallimard, 1957, p. 270.
13. Preface to *La Montagne Ensorcelée*, Paris, Editeurs Français Réunis, (1972 edn).
14. *Reflets D'Haiti*, 7, November 1955, p. 8.
15. *Présence Africaine*, 13, May 1957, p. 100.
16. *The Historical Novel*, Harmondsworth, Peregrine, 1969, p. 44.
17. *Présence Africaine*, 8–10, June–November 1956, p. 260.
18. *Romancero aux étoiles*, Paris, Gallimard, 1960, p. 201.

NOTE

Senghor's Verse

Jeannette Kamara

In her article 'Senghor Re-evaluated' (*African Literature Today*, No. 6, p. 58), Julia di Stefano Pappageorge states that the following line from Senghor's poem 'Nuit de Sine'

> Dodelinent de la tête comme l'enfant sur le dos de sa mère

is a dactylic pentameter. I would like to point out that the dactylic penta- meter does not exist in French prosody which is based on syllabic count as opposed to the metre of English verse. The metre of French prosody is, if anything, more akin to the iamb and/or the anapaest. The tonic accent generally falls on the last syllable of a word or group of words, the syntagma, following the patterns of the spoken language. To quote Grammont:

> Il n'y a qu'un principe admissible pour le compte de syllabes: se conformer le plus possible à la prononciation de la langue vivante.[1]

> (There is only one principle admissible for the count of syllables: to follow as closely as possible the pronunciation of the spoken language.)

This line, or rather verset, is composed of two syntagma or word groups separated by the caesura, or pause, after the word 'tête'. The final or mute 'e' is not counted, falling as it does at the pause at the end of the word group. The line should thus be scanned in the following manner:

7/10 Dodelínent de la tête // comme l'enfant sur le dos de sa mère.

The verset is composed of a seven-syllable followed by a ten-syllable group, with the accent falling on the third and seventh syllables in the first group, on the fourth, seventh, and tenth syllables of the second group. It is typical of the Senghorian verset which is generally in two parts, each with an even syllabic count respecting the rules of French prosody: hexasyllabic, octosyllabic, decasyllabic, dodecasyllabic. The poet often uses an uneven syllabic unit within this binary infrastructure for purposes of emphasis. Senghor, talking about his art, writes:

J'ai voulu (pour cela), partir de la versification française, en respectant les principes naturels, c'est-à-dire le génie de la langue française.[2]

(I wanted (. . .), to use French prosody as a starting point, respecting its natural principles, that is to say, the genius of the French language.)

And elsewhere:

En général, mes vers blancs sont binaires et comportent un nombre de syllabes pair . . . Il arrive cependant, assez souvent, que j'emploie un vers blanc composé d'un nombre de syllabes impair. C'est, en principe, pour obtenir un effet caractéristique . . .[2]

(In general, my blank verse is binary and contains an even number of syllables . . . However, it happens, quite frequently, that I use blank verse composed of an uneven number of syllables. This is done, as a rule, to obtain a particular effect.)

About his use of the diphthong he writes:

En ce qui conerne la diphthongue, j'en ai usé comme on en use aujour d'hui dans le parler courant. J'en ai fait, en général, une seule syllabe.[2]

(Concerning the diphthong, I have used it as it is used today in current speech. I have, on the whole, made it a single syllable.)

The uneven syllabic count of the first syntagma of the verset in question effectively draws attention to and thus emphasizes the nodding movement of the drowsy story-tellers. The line is best appreciated within the verse which scans thus:

10–7   Voici que décline la lune lasse // vers son lit de mer étale

12/6   Voici que s'assoupissent les éclats de rire // que les conteurs
        eux-mêmes

7/10   Dodelinent de la tête // comme l'enfant sur le dos de sa mère

11/12   Voici que les pieds des danseurs s'alourdissent, // que
        s'alourdit la langue des choeurs alternés.

NOTES

1. M. Grammont, *Petit traité de versification française*, Paris, Armand Colin, Collection U, 1965, p. 19.
2. Senghor, in a letter to Sylvia B. Â., October 1967.

REVIEWS

Cyprian Ekwensi and
Albert von Haller (eds)
Moderne Erzähler der Welt: Nigeria

Willfried Feuser

Cyprian Ekwensi and Albert von Haller (eds), *Moderne Erzähler der Welt: Nigeria*, translated by Albert von Haller, Tübingen and Basel, Horst Erdmann Verlag, 1973.

From I. N. C. Aniebo's 'The Dilemma', published in *Nigeria Magazine*, 79, 1963, to Gabriel Okara's 'The Laughing Ghost', which appeared in the maiden issue of *Oduma*, a publication of the Rivers State Council for Arts and Culture, in October 1973, this German anthology covers ten years of Nigerian story telling.

The contributors' narrative technique ranges from the traditional (Fagunwa, in Soyinka's translation; Tutucla; and Gbadamosi) to the modern (Ekwensi; Achebe; Owoyele). Some stories skirt the experimental genre, like Femi Euba's 'The Meaning of the Whole', in which a Nigerian student in London anticipates his marriage to an English girl at the subconscious level, and Obotunde Ijimere's 'Clanking Horseman in the Heat of Day', a story, told with subtle irony, dealing with the 'conversion' of a young Englishman hunting for sacred images by the mystical power of a Yoruba priest.

It is an open secret that Obotunde Ijimere is the pen-name of Ulli Beier, who has also contributed a superb German rendering of Bakare Gbadamosi's moral tale 'He who takes too much into his mouth must see how he can swallow it' to the collection.

Sometimes hilarious (Frank Aig Imoukhuede, David Owoyele) and sometimes haunting (M. J. C. Echeruo with 'Uchegwu's Song'), the volume is beautifully produced and presented with a sensitive introduction by Albert von Haller.

Some textual errors could have been avoided by a closer co-operation between the Nigerian editor and his German counterpart and translator, who apparently had to fight a running battle with Nigerian pidgin, e.g. in Chinua Achebe's short story. 'Civil Peace' ('I de ask you say you wan make we call soldier?'), and with such deceptively simple expressions as 'pepper soup' or even 'biro'.

In the introduction to the book Yetunde Esan is changed into a man (p. 30), while in the notes Vincent Chukwuemeka Ike, who before taking over responsibility for the West African Examinations Council gave us an insider's view of the workings of a University administration in Africa in his novel, *The Naked Gods*, is transferred from the registry to the post of archivist at Nsukka (p. 34) and Gabriel Okara is prematurely elevated to the ministerial rank denied Miss Flora Nwapa (p. 350). An index stating the sources of the material used would considerably enhance the value of the book.

A Tale of Tamed Tigers

Willfried Feuser

Martin Steins, *Das Bild des Schwarzen in der europäischen Kolonialliteratur. Ein Beitrag zur literarischen Imagologie 1870–1918*, Frankfurt a.M., Thesen Verlag, 1972.

This study by a young Belgian scholar is based on the assumption formulated by the *comparatiste*, Marius F. Guyard: 'Given the right method, one can describe exactly the image or images of a country having currency in another country during a particular period.' It deals with the genesis, development, and impact, both literary and social, of the black man's image in the white man's mind. Although purportedly restricted to European literature on Africa from the outbreak of the Franco-Prussian War to the end of the First World War, it considerably overshoots the target date in a brilliant discussion linking the image thus formed to the gyrations of the European mind between the two World Wars on the one hand, and the Negritude movement on the other. Far from merely reflecting those human stereotypes which have taken shape in public opinion at large, literature is here shown to create, and propagate, such stereotypes, which tend to be of greater importance in the assessment of one national or racial group by another than the outgroup's objectively observable behaviour. Moreover, the author heightens our awareness of the fact that the stereotyped image created by a literature often tells us more about the irrational fears and desires of the image-maker than about the social group it purports to define.

According to Dr Steins, the image of Africa (geographical) and of the African (anthropological) between 1870 and 1918 developed in two distinct phases. The first phase was that of exoticism, epitomized in the works of Pierre Loti (*Le Roman d'un spahi*, 1881) and Paul Vigné d'Octon (*Terre de Mort*, 1892), whose Africa is a fever-infested land of death, the white man's grave, spelling sterility, physical degradation, and moral decline; its image of man, informed by the Hamitic myth and Joseph de Maistre's view of the 'homme dégénéré et puni' is one of degeneracy and savagery; its political outlook anti-colonialist. The second phase brought about Africa's transformation into a 'virgin land' full of primeval vigour, 'a fountain of youth' in the words of Ernest Psichari, the French colonial officer in quest of the promised land – 'un des derniers refuges de l'énergie nationale' – where, after the defeat of 1871, France might redeem herself. This second phase, unashamedly colonialist, endeavours to make Africa look more attractive. It draws its image of man from Gobineau. The tired degenerate cradling a death-wish in lustreless eyes is succeeded by the 'primitive', a raw human specimen with unequalled gifts of rhythm and artistic emotion. Strangely fascinated by him, and wary of his own machine-made civilization, the colonial administrator now bestrides the scene, proudly proclaiming himself a bushman ('broussard') – a tough mixture of noble savage and Nietzschean *Übermensch*.

In between the two phases, and not fitting into either pattern, we find a small group of non-conformist writers. About twenty years before Frobenius' sojourn at Ibadan and Ife the French traveller Jean Hess, convalescing in Oyo, the capital of Yorubaland, after an attack by hostile Bariba tribesmen, discovered the greatness of antiquity, the graciousness of Old Testament times, in a traditional African society. His 'Bible Nègre', dictated to him by the Alafin's court historian but for some curious reason classified by Steins as a 'short story', is probably the first comprehensive account of Yoruba mythology published in any European language. Hess included it in his book, *L'Ame nègre* (1898), whose title is akin to Du Bois' *The Souls of Black Folk* (1903) and anticipates the 'discovery' of the Negro soul by Delafosse.

The first coherent image of the Negro – flashing teeth, hilarious laughter, dionysian rhythm, and animaline strength, 'a domesticated tiger drunk on the smell of gunpowder' fighting unthinkingly for the glory of France when thrust on to European battlefields – is thus essentially the creation of the second phase, or 'littérature coloniale'. Disengaged from the vague cliché of exotic non-European peoples in general that obtained in previous centuries, and merging with the vitalistic image of the Harlem jazzman, it acquired an increasingly positive complexion in the anti-intellectual, irrationalist climate of such movements as Dadaism, Expressionism, and Surrealism, and found its final apotheosis in Negritude, via writers like René Maran (*Batouala*, 1921), Maurice Delafosse (*L'Ame nègre*, 1922), and Paul Morand (*Magie noire*, 1927).

Ironically, one of Field-Marshal Joffre's tamed tigers, the Fulani rifleman Bakary Diallo, who had his jaw shattered by German shrapnel on the Marne, became the first twentieth-century African writer in French worthy of note. Despite his naive worship of the power and the goodness that was France he was passionately concerned about the rehabilitation of the blacks 'among the races of the world – *savages all*' (*Force-Bonté*, 1926, p. 123).

Dr Steins's analysis cuts deep and makes other comparatively recent studies, e.g. Léon Fanoudh-Siefer's *La mythe du nègre et de l'Afrique Noire dans la littérature française* (1968), seem dated. He points to the fact that 'la littérature coloniale', to which the major part of his study is devoted, is but the ideological superstructure of economic and political forces. African researchers who may wish to venture into the field, following in the foot-steps of J. M. Abanda Ndengue (Yaoundé) or E. C. Nwezeh (Ife), whose doctoral thesis on *L'Afrique Noire dans les littératures française et allemande depuis Agadir jusqu'à l'arrivée de Hitler au pouvoir* (Paris, 1974) applies the comparative approach to a more recent period, cannot afford to bypass Steins's work. Its only major flaw is the author's *a priori* assertion that the French image of Africa is representative of the whole of Europe. Although some space is devoted to Joseph Conrad, the Belgian Jef Geeraerts, the Italian futurist Marinetti, and German expressionist poets evoking the Negro's image, one feels that vast areas of the kaleidoscope of European opinion on African have been dismissed offhand and that a more encyclopaedic approach, taking into account such works as V. N. McCullough's *The Negro in English Literature* (1962), G. D. Killam's *Africa in English Fiction* (1968), Louis Morales Oliver's *Africa en la literatura española* (1957–8), and Gerald Moser's findings on Portuguese colonial literature would have been indicated. But this would doubtless have exploded the book's capacity of 250 tightly packed pages, including its rare and ambitious bibliography.

Sembene Ousmane
Xala

Maryse Condé

Sembene Ousmane, *Xala*, London, Heinemann, African Writers Series No. 175, 1976.

Sembene Ousmane is an exception in French-speaking West Africa. He is almost the only writer who started publishing novels during the colonial period, and still does, denouncing the evils of the post-independence era as he did for pre-independence. He is the only one who, realizing the limitations of literature, especially literature written in French in largely illiterate societies, turned to another medium and made several films, thus becoming a pioneer in the field of African cinema. More important even, in our countries where the prestige of the so-called intellectual is so great, he constantly refused to be more than a man of the people close to his roots.

Xala is his last novel, first published in 1974 by *Présence Africaine* and already released as a film. In fact the release of the film in his native Senegal brought a few problems to Sembene. He was asked to cut out a few scenes considered too offensive for the French presence and although it became afterwards the opportunity for a 'soirée de gala' at the Daniel Sorano theatre in Dakar, the intrigues were many. *Xala* is set in Dakar, since the Senegalese society is what Sembene Ousmane seems to know best. The hero, El Hadji Abdou Kader Beye, belongs to the new class born after independence. He is a businessman just nominated as the Head of the Chamber of Commerce and Industry, the first Senegalese to occupy this seat. As the crowning of his happiness, he decides to marry a third wife, the young N'Gone. The story opens with the description of the wedding party, complete with male and female griots, champagne, and expensive gifts. As well as a car, El Hadji has promised 2,500 gallons of petrol to the new bride. The two other wives are also present at the ceremony and portrayed with great skill by Sembene Ousmane who makes us aware of their different personalities through their behaviour in the circumstances. But on his wedding night, El Hadji up to now so fortunate, discovers he has the *xala* – which means that he is suddenly impotent. This impotency is the writing on the wall. It is not only his physical manhood which is at stake, but his dignity and even his wealth. In his desperate attempts to cure his disease, he neglects his business which goes from bad to worse since in fact El Hadji was just a pretence of a businessman, living on credit and with no real financial power. This is in my point of view the most striking aspect of Sembene Ousmane's novel: the constant criticism, the constant demythification of the characters and aspects of society. In the end El Hadji's driver, Modu, proposes to take him to a very good marabout who lives up-country and El Hadji can only accept. The journey is an exhausting one reminding us of these quests which abound in oral traditions.

Beneath the torrid heat of the sun nature was covered with a thin layer of greyish dust, streaked by the rough tongue of the wind. The landscape was marked by a grandiose, calm austerity and harmony.

Sereen Mada, when they reach him at last, is a holy man surrounded by his disciples and he effectively cures El Hadji. As a payment for his services, El Hadji gives him a cheque and goes back to Dakar. To tell the end of the story in detail would not be fair. Let us say only that El Hadji will soon get his *xala* back and will have to look for a final cure. He eventually finds it in the last pages of the book where he goes through an extraordinary ordeal. His first wife Adja Awa Astou remains with him as everybody else has deserted him, especially the new young wife whom he could never possess.

The story is told on two levels. First it is a devastating satire of the new Senegalese bourgeoisie, greedy, selfish, and basically unable to create anything great and lasting. Its petty desires revolve around cars, women, and a few titles for prestige. It feeds itself with the crumbs left over from the former masters and its nationalism, its cry for Africanization, are just a way of getting its hands on power. Women as well as men are attacked, since two of El Hadji's wives are shallow creatures merely interested in his money.

But although Sembene Ousmane, basically a realist, might deny this interpretation, *Xala* goes far beyond the frontiers of Senegal. It is Africa as a whole which cannot produce anything fruitful, as its elites and leaders are oblivious of the masses, of their needs and despair. The tragedy of El Hadji owes its dimensions to another tragedy, the one of a continent betrayed by its own sons. The solution, since there is a solution as Sembene Ousmane is not a pessimist, lies in mending the present class disparities; not only reconciliation, but the submission of the so-called elites to the poor and the destitute, to those who never had their say in politics. El Hadji Kader Beye recovers his health when the beggars and the cripples have washed his sins with their spittle, when he has shed his pride and impudence.

Africa will certainly get off to a new start when those in power have renounced their futile privileges.

Ekwensi and Okpewho on the Nigerian Civil War

Kadiatu Sesay

Cyprian Ekwensi, *Survive the Peace*, London, Heinemann, African Writers Series No. 185, 1976; Isidore Okpewho, *The Last Duty*, London, Longman, 1976.

Cyprian Ekwensi's *Survive the Peace* and Isidore Okpewho's *The Last Duty*, in their different ways, present the devastating effects of the Nigerian civil war on the lives of individuals. *Survive the Peace* portrays atrocities and personal tragedies which indelibly marked the lives of those who, even when they escaped actual death in the war, became vulnerable to the violence of peace. James Odugo, a radio-journalist, having survived the war, faces an even greater battle to survive 'the peace'. Separated from his wife and children, he discovers at the end of the war that his marriage and the integrity of his family life have been totally destroyed. The 'last duty' of Okpewho's title is not a man's patriotic duty to fight and die for his tribe or country but his obligation to suffer manfully for his personal ideals of justice and honour. The hero, having suffered unjustly throughout the war, finds that peace brings no comfort either.

Ekwensi's *Survive the Peace* is a fairly interesting documentary providing some poignant individual episodes of the resultant suffering, but these episodes are not organized into an artistic whole as Okpewho, a more accomplished craftsman, manages to do. Ekwensi always has a great amount of information for the reader; his problem is lack of art. While the art of a good novelist is to show rather than tell, Ekwensi most of the time tells rather than shows, as here, where he tells the reader where the post-war armed bandits got their arms:

> They [defeated rebel soldiers] ... were disrobing and changing into civilian clothes ... Hundreds more began ... flinging their guns. Odugo noticed that some villagers ... were picking up these guns and ammunition and running into the trees with them. The world was later to hear of prowling groups of armed bandits holding up travellers on the Nigerian highways ... (pp. 10–11)

This is journalism rather than the novelist's art.

Survive the Peace is a string of episodes some of which conflict with others for no artistic reason and although each episode is meant to portray life as it really is, many of them are unconvincingly portrayed and do not spring from much psychological insight or power of characterization. Samson Ukoha, facing the prospect of sudden death from an overwhelming enemy force, removes his hat and delivers an incredibly long 'prayer' giving us in the process what appears to be Ekwensi's reflections on the war. Samson even manages to include the consoling point that Nigeria is not unique in fighting a civil war; the Germans, the British, and the Americans have all, at some stage in history, fought similar wars. No doubt the purpose is to pass on the implicitly optimistic message that, if these countries have survived, so too will Nigeria – Ekwensi more explicitly builds this optimistic message on to the end of the novel. The ideas in this speech, looked at in isolation, are quite sane, but in the mouth of a soldier facing almost certain and swift death – as a last prayer – they become absurd and unconvincing. No soldier in such circumstances would spend his time moralizing instead of fighting or running away. Nor is Ekwensi being ironical; on the contrary he is portraying the dedicated soldier who, even on the verge of death, cares for the welfare of his army and country. Samson is described by the soldier who took his body home as 'one who fought like a true son of Obodonta'.

The end of the novel is melodramatic, unconvincing, and shows either haste or lack of care. With Pa Ukoha's illness, Ekwensi effects a miraculous coincidence whereby all the old man's children, Kalu, a medical doctor from Germany, Abel, a computer scientist from somewhere else, Christopher, an accountant with a construction company in America, Francis, a priest, and Ngozi, all pour into his compound at the same time. Ada, the old man's wife, comes in and announces their extraordinary arrival thus: 'Pa the children are back from the war.' What war could Ada possibly be talking about here? Or has the author himself forgotten what he said on the same page that these children 'had all changed with the years away from these shores ... And they had seen nothing of the war'? (p. 176).

Determined to produce a happy ending with a message of optimism for the Nigerian future, the author has to make sure that Pa Ukoha is preserved and is reunited with his scattered family regardless of the cost in credibility. The fairy-tale ending is topped with a symbol of hope in the form of a new-born child called Nkiruka meaning, 'that which lies ahead is greater'. There is nothing wrong with the author's good intentions; only his art is deficient.

The Last Duty, Okpewho's second novel, is a very accomplished performance. He brings out the attitudes of his main characters – each narrating the events of the novel from their own point of view – 'to the themes of honour, conscience, personal good and self-respect'. Thus the main events are described more than once; but these different narrations, far from being merely repetitive, create tension, suspense, and interest, show the characters through other eyes, and deepen the significance of the main events.

Okpewho's psychological penetration and power of characterization are impressive, his main characters fully developed and convincing. The individual motivations and often conflicting interests come out so well that the author has no need to pass judgment on their weaknesses and follies; we can see why they behave the way they do.

Toje Onovwakpo, a boastful, big rubber plantation owner, in his own eyes one of the most important men in Urukpe, trumps up charges of collaboration with the rebels against his rival rubber planter, Mukoro Oshevire, who is consequently put in detention. Okpewho's portrayal of the egotistic, pompous, and self-opinionated Toje is well done, for he not only brings out Toje's villainy but makes him, like Iago in *Othello*, cast about for motives to make his evil presentable to himself. Neither the author nor his readers will agree with Toje's perverted and tilted logic as he papers over his own treachery:

> I am a big man ... This town has people like me to thank for what notice it has achieved today ... That's why I have not hesitated to recommend a citizen here for detention on charges for collaboration with the rebels ... For I felt that Mukoro ... stood in my way. And that again is why I have not hesitated to seek carnal pleasure with his forlorn wife now that I feel my manhood flawed, my potency questioned ... And what town is there that can survive if it becomes known that one of its most pre-eminent citizens has no claim to manhood? (p. 5)

Toje's tortured rationalizing is portrayed through a careful choice of words. He has not fabricated charges against Oshevire; he has merely 'recommended' him for detention – much more self-justifying – and 'seek carnal pleasure' is a much more self-protecting periphrasis than his sordid tactics.

The same careful characterization is shown in the portrayal of the other characters. Aku, Oshevire's wife, tells her story with honesty and conscience. The main impression one gets of her is that of a loving and dedicated wife prepared to stand by her husband in the face of difficulties. The crux of the novel shows her moral defeat when her dormant sexual emotions are tickled and activated by the impotent villain, Toje, to such an extreme that she is eventually reduced to inviting Odibo, Toje's crippled nephew and unwilling go-between, to supply the physical satisfaction which Toje could not provide. The odds are stacked high against Aku. Trapped in the hostile town of the Igabos, with her husband in detention, she is assailed by hostile eyes from all sides. She cannot even venture to the market to buy food for her child and herself without running this gauntlet of hostility. Time and suffering, in the absence of a husband or even a friend, reduce her to a state of non-resistance to the wishes of Toje. She had the alternatives of either giving in to his demands and at least getting food in order to stay alive with her son and vindicating her husband's honour, or standing firm in the name of chastity and starving to death with the child. She blames herself for falling the way she does and this honesty, this self-confession, must be borne in mind in judging her.

To Oshevire, Aku's husband in detention, his last duty is clear; it is to 'vindicate the cause of justice, and, even if they succeed in taking your life in the end, prove to them all too clearly that theirs was an idle victory for your honesty towers tall and superior above everything, like a wild palm, tough and upright' (p. 33). The tragedy lies not so much in the fall of Aku but in the destruction of a man of such sterling character as Oshevire. He returns to Urukpe from detention to discover not only that his wife has been unfaithful but that Toje and Odibo have half-killed each other in a jealous fight over her. The spiritual basis of his home life has been destroyed; he completes the process by destroying the physical manifestations.

In the portrayal of Odibo and Oghenovo, the 5-year-old son of Aku and Oshevire, Okpewho shows subtle characterization through his use of different registers. Odibo, Toje's crippled nephew and messenger to Aku, at first uses a style which reflects his lack of confidence in his own powers: 'I know I am not worth much or anything. I know I cannot help myself or anybody. I cannot think or do anything.' The style of short, simple sentences illustrates a man whose mental ability cannot accommodate complexity. He finds it difficult to unravel the mystery surrounding Toje's meetings with Aku in his house because he lacks the confidence to face the facts. His style however changes as he is 'transformed to a man' towards the end of the novel by Aku's 'love'. His sentences become more complex: 'At once he throws his entire rage on me unleashing both hands one after the other in blinding blows on my face; cursing, spitting, even kicking me with his legs . . .' (p. 213).

Okpewho's artistry in the choice of language for his characters also comes out in his portrayal of Oghenovo. As a child, he cannot comprehend most of the things that happen and he tells his own version of the story with the innocence and limitations of a child of his age. His style is rambling (aptly represented without capital letters); his sentences are a piling up of repetitive phrases and clauses linked together by simple conjunctions, each sentence consisting of a whole incident and sometimes more than one.

and then i came home, and my mother asked me where i had gone, and i told her that i went to show onome my clothes and that onome said my father was a thief and did not buy me any clothes, because he was a prisoner and the soldiers had put him into prison because, because, he had stolen something that belonged to them and my mother said . . . (p. 15)

Even though this is only Okpewho's second novel – unlike Ekwensi who has written many – he has come out as a more mature and resourceful artist whose characters are well developed and convincing; he shows a great ability to describe episodes in appropriate prose, and sustains the reader's interest with his skilful use of different narrative styles, throughout this substantial novel.

Omunjakko Nakibimbiri
The Sobbing Sounds

Kadiatu Sesay

Omunjakko Nakibimbiri, *The Sobbing Sounds*, London, Longman, 1976.

Omunjakko Nakibimbiri's *The Sobbing Sounds* is an addition to the 'anti-hero' type of writing which has now become popular particularly in East Africa. Unlike the Okonkwos and the Ezeulus, conservative heroes who stand firm for the established norms of their societies and who are destroyed while fighting to prevent changes from infiltrating them, the anti-hero is a rebel, sometimes only a passive one, who does nothing heroic and rejects the established norms of his society. This anti-heroic type of writing is exemplified by Okot P'Bitek's *Song of Malaya*, in which the prostitute, instead of being accused by society, turns round and castigates that society for contributing in making her a 'malaya'. In Nakibimbiri's novel, Kabaliga is this type of non-conformist anti-hero:

> . . . I wondered what the hell I, 'a man of letters' was doing in Kivvulu where I did not belong? . . . Why the hell did I have to succumb to the loving wiles of Maaso, whose residence was in the slums, when there were Betty, Cathy, Milly, Maggie, all fellow graduates of mine? Was my education all gone to waste? This education – how did it start, and how did education shape my social life, including this vital activity called sex? How did I come to honour girls and women who knew what the 'sobbing sounds' meant to sex? Girls like Maaso and her slum-dwelling illiterate compatriates? (pp. 4–5)

The rest of the novel is an answer to these questions – an impenitent reconstruction of Kabaliga's early life and how it influenced his sexual greed.

From his first lessons at the hands of his rather free-living cousin, Matama, through a variety of surreptitious viewing sessions on the sexual encounters of parents, teachers, and friends, sex and the accompanying sobbing sounds came to occupy a central part of his psychology. Voyeurism led to participation and from his somewhat expert position, Kabaliga comments on the sexual behaviour of Ugandan and Western women and, importantly for him, Westernized Ugandan women who are, to him, inferior to the unspoiled Ugandans.

At first glance, one may be tempted to call this straight pornography, but it is not; Nakibimbiri is making an important and valid point: that the kinds of sexual experience gone through by Kabaliga could lead one to become what Kabaliga is – a man who runs after sex for its own sake with a somewhat perverted taste. The author is in no way condoning the Kabaligas or 'malayas' of Uganda, but has endeavoured to show some of the social causes that lead to their existence. He shows how society casts out on the one hand, girls like Nakibote, who lose their chastity and therefore their marriage price, by forcing them into loveless marriages, and on the other, girls like Ayisa Nabuzaana who 'had been forced by her father to marry a man who was not her choice' and who ran away to Kampala and prostitution.

In a superficially unserious and apparently simple novel, Nakibimbiri has succeeded in highlighting, very frankly, some of the serious social problems of his society in a narrative style well suited to this theme. The frequent digressions may be distracting but, in general, they accord with the free and easy character of the anti-hero.

Two Views of Urban Life:
Meja Mwangi, *Going Down River Road*
Nuruddin Farah, *A Naked Needle*

Eustace Palmer

Meja Mwangi, *Going Down River Road*, London, Heinemann, African Writers Series No. 176, 1976; Nuruddin Farah, *A Naked Needle*, London, Heinemann, African Writers Series No. 184, 1976.

It would be a remarkable twist of fate if Cyprian Ekwensi, despite all his artistic flaws, proves to have had a more decisive influence on the contemporary African novel than Chinua Achebe. Ekwensi's *forte* is the analysis of the social realities in the new African urban aggregations, and the recent publication of a number of such novels suggests that this is one of the major preoccupations of contemporary African novelists. The Kenyan Meja Mwangi is certainly one of the most exciting of these new East African writers. He is already the author of two successful novels, *Kill Me Quick* and *Carcase for Hounds*, in which he amply demonstrated his characteristic qualities – a touching compassion for the social or political underdog, a quietness of tone which emphasizes rather than obscures the very serious problems being analysed, and a remarkably controlled though unpretentious prose style.

Mwangi's latest novel, *Going Down River Road*, displays all these characteristics. Set in Nairobi's seething brothel, pub, and cheap nightclub area, the novel presents with commendable power and detailed demonstration the fortunes of the hero, Ben, against the background of all those social forces which we have now come to associate with the growth of modern African cities. Mwangi hits on the clever device of using the framework of the construction of the luxurious twenty-four-storey Development Building as a means of presenting the experiences of the ordinary workers whose life-styles are in such stark contrast with all that that Development Building represents, but who must look forward to the completion of the building with apprehension since it would mean the loss of their jobs. Mwangi's exploration of urban problems is if anything, more detailed, more sensitive, and ultimately more convincing than anything that Ekwensi has ever written. The squalor, degradation, and misery are tellingly presented through case histories such as that of Wini, Ben's girlfriend who had a child at the age of 14 and was forced into prostitution to keep herself and the fatherless child, but still possessed enough moral courage to see her through a secretarial course. She eventually gets a decent job but is forced to abandon her baby and elope with her boss as a way out of the urban impasse. There is the 16-year-old prostitute who fornicates with Ben in the same room in which her friend is simultaneously having fun with another man while her month-old baby screams in the corner. Such scenes give convincing social motivations of conduct while generating tremendous sympathy for the unfortunates who are trapped in the situation. Far from being titillating, the sexual details stamp unforgettably on the reader's mind the hopelessness of the masses in the struggle to survive. The prostitutes are dogged by a basic insecurity and the fear of hunger; the fun-loving teenage girls who are hired out by their boyfriends are so vulnerable to the sadistic whims of drunkards, thugs, and drug-addicts. Indeed, violence is never far from the surface. It degenerates quite often into motiveless hatred and even murder. The inhabitants of the River Road area occasionally demonstrate a certain comradeship in adversity and the reader is made to experience the warmth of populist amusement-spots such as Eden or the Karara centre, but he still senses the absence of real friendship which is ultimately attributable to the dehumanizing effect of the impersonal city where everyone is involved in the scramble to survive. Mwangi does not flinch from presenting the grim realities of the housing racket, the corruption of the politicians, the high cost of living and its consequences, and organized as well as petty crime.

Mwangi's preoccupation with the social realities of the city does not prevent him from creating some interesting characters and exploring some significant relationships. The hero, Ben, is the most fascinating of them all. A central consciousness through whose eyes almost all the events and the other characters are viewed, he survives in the mind of the reader as a kind of anti-hero whose huge bulk and physical strength go oddly with his lack of resolution and real guts. There is even a slight hint of some kind of emasculation in this young man who, in spite of his sexual prowess, seems unable to father his own child or have a lasting relationship with a woman and at the end adopts a child who everyone knows to have been fathered by another man.

His story is one of progressive deterioration from the initial disgrace when, succumbing very easily to a gangster's temptation, he is expelled from the army and then loses his cosy insurance job. Robbed thus of self-respect and strength of will, he merely drifts from one casual job to another until the educated, one-time lieutenant ends up as a casual labourer on a building construction site. He meets Wini the prostitute and decides to move in with her and her 4-year-old son, but Wini is obviously the dominant person in the household. When it suits her purpose she leaves, abandoning her son, Baby, to Ben, as though she were the father and he the mother. Subsequently the landlord ejects him from the flat on the pretext that it has been rented to Wini. Ben is thus forced to move into his friend Ocholla's makeshift shanty-hut with all the squalor and degradation that that involves. And when Ocholla's enormous family turns up unexpectedly from the provinces all the signs suggest that Ben and Baby will be turned out homeless once more.

Yet for all his weakness we are always aware of Ben's compassion for his fellow sufferers. His touching relationships with Ocholla and little Baby are fascinating. At the start Ben is repelled by Baby's unfortunate habits. But when his mother absconds, the reader watches, fascinated, as Ben gradually comes to accept responsibility for the boy and to care for him, effectively playing the roles of both father and mother. At the end both

Ocholla and Ben, who have been rather aimless drifters for most of the novel, come to accept the lessons of responsibility; just as Ben accepts responsibility for Baby, so Ocholla accepts responsibility for his large family whom he has completely neglected in the provinces. This acquisition of wider relationships is perhaps the most convincing ray of hope held out in the novel; for with it both men begin to regain their self-respect. As Ben, now playing the role of a responsible father, begins to tell Baby, who has been playing truant, of the difference between right and wrong and the need for decent living, the real man in him emerges and we think that he more than deserves his promotion to the post of foreman.

Mwangi's earthy language matches the status and occupations of his characters, but it is perhaps inexcusable for him to lapse into it himself in his own narrative. Perhaps Wini's character could also have been more fully developed. One finds it rather unconvincing that the girl who had shown so much fondness for her only child would abandon it unceremoniously without any thought of ever seeing it again. But these are small faults in a novel which is unmistakably an accomplished achievement.

Nuruddin Farah's *The Naked Needle* similarly presents the experiences of a disillusioned young man against the background of social and political corruption in a largely urban area, this time Somalia's capital, Mogadiscio. The novel is technically exciting. Where Mwangi eschews formal innovations, contenting himself instead with the presentation of his characters' experiences in depth, Farah makes copious use of flashbacks and reminiscences interspersing the dialogue. The reminiscences are largely those of the hero Koschin who, like Ben in *Going Down River Road*, functions as a central consciousness through whose eyes the reader views the decadence of contemporary Mogadiscio. Koschin emerges as a determined if rather confused revolutionary. The reader is struck by his moral idealism and his determination not to succumb to authoritarianism. But it is a measure of the difference between these two novels that, whereas Ben is solidly realized, Koschin remains a shadowy figure for all his reminiscences. The problem is that Farah relies much more on statement and assertion than on demonstration or dramatic presentation. In consequence Farah's Mogadiscio is much less vividly presented than Mwangi's Nairobi. Indeed the reader is very likely to forget that he is being presented with a picture of an urban environment. There is certainly comment on city life; there is a hint of the absurdity of bureaucracy, the corruption of politicians, the squalor of the masses, ministerial incompetence, nepotism, and the destructiveness of the city; but it is all done on the level of statement and not of demonstration.

On a first reading it might superficially appear that the poverty of the urban presentation may be due to Farah's greater interest in human relationships, specifically, the relationship between men and women or between black men and their white women in independent Africa. Three such relationships are given. There is that between Koschin's friend Barre and his American wife, which comes to grief because it is based on lies and neither is prepared to make allowances; there is the successful relationship between another friend Mohamed and his wife Barbara which is due to a complete understanding and acceptance of each other's nature and a determination to be flexible; and there is Koschin's relationship with Nancy which is eventually successful because they have both been quite honest with each other. But apart from the Mohamed-Barbara marriage, none of these relationships is convincingly presented. Most importantly, we fail to experience the process whereby Koschin, who was quite detached from and rather irritated by Nancy at the start, gradually comes closer to her and accepts her at the end. The fact is that Farah is much too pre-occupied with mere social comment to be interested in scenes or in people. There is an attempt at a Soyinka-like scenic presentation at a party given by one of Koschin's friends, but it fails to come to life. Attempts at a kind of poetic intensity backfire similarly. Nuruddin Farah's second novel is interesting but not entirely satisfactory.

Ernest N. Emenyonu
Cyprian Ekwensi

Charles E. Nnolim

Ernest N. Emenyonu, *Cyprian Ekwensi*, London, Evans Brothers, 1974.

Dr Emenyonu's *Cyprian Ekwensi* can only enhance his growing stature as a critic of African literature. But any review of his present book must not overlook that controversial article of his entitled 'African Literature: What Does It Take To Be Its Critic?' (*African Literature Today*, No. 5, 1971) in which he took Bernth Lindfors to task for his earlier article on Ekwensi (in *ALT*, No. 3, 1969). While Emenyonu's article was admittedly a one-sided *apologia* for Ekwensi's works, the present volume shows considerable signs of maturity and a critical sense of balance. Emenyonu now examines Ekwensi's canon with the cold critical eye of a scientist who feels he has a job to do: the sentimental attachment has disappeared, and devotion to truth has replaced the earlier overprotective attachment to Ekwensi whom he had thought of as a writer much maligned by expatriate critics who did not fully understand his art.

I would begin, impiously, with the flaws in this book. There is a confusion in the use of literary terms. Instead of making the simple modern distinctions between the short story, the novelette, and the novel, Emenyonu gets trapped into using the oldfashioned term *novella* so that the reader never knows when the author means short story and when he means short novel. And one must point out that the plural of *novella* is not *novellas* as the author uses the term, but *novelle*.

Owing to no fault of the author's, the first twenty-eight pages of the book are cluttered unnecessarily: title page, Ekwensi's portrait, Gerald Moore's manifesto for the Modern African Writers Series, author's dedicatory note, another note on critical works published under the series, table of contents, About the Author (incredibly repeated on the back cover), acknowledgments, Preface, author's Introduction – all these the reader must wade through before the business of the book really begins.

The author's own organization of the book leaves much to be desired. First of all, the Introduction is actually a misnomer. It should have been entitled 'Cyprian Ekwensi: A Biographical Sketch'. As a biographical sketch it is well researched and is quite revealing of Ekwensi, the man, influences on his writing, the versatility of his talents, and how he normally operates as a writer. His actual temperament as a fallible human being is only muted in the Freudian slip: 'Ekwensi is a *fast* and conscientious man' (my italics). The major weakness of this chapter is in its organization. The last paragraph goes into a jarring summary-statement about Ekwensi's 'weaknesses', 'major concerns', and 'maturity' as a writer, *before* the author even begins to acquaint the reader with Ekwensi's works. Secondly, the last paragraph seems out of place in what has been all along a biographical sketch. What this false step does is to leave the author with no summary-statement (born out of the findings of the book) at the end. To fill this vacuum, the author's last chapter, his 'Conclusion', is left with no critical statement to make; instead he quotes a lengthy and angry letter written by Ekwensi to an equally angry Anamelechi. This angry letter (actually revelatory of Ekwensi's temperament) could easily switch places with the last paragraph of the 'Introduction'.

The Preface declares Ekwensi a writer of much controversy and avows to fill a gap in Ekwensi scholarship by tracing Ekwensi's literary growth as a writer. This, in itself, is admirable. But the author seems to have no declared methodology, no consistent method of analysis, no plan of attack, no hypothesis to be tested, hence no urge in his 'Conclusion' to make a summary statement as to the success or failure of his own critical quest. In the end, one must admit, by some sort of 'positive skewing', the author seems to have covered more critical ground by not having a declared (and constricting) thesis to trap him.

Finally, there are some typographical errors and a few solecisms to be pointed out: Iyi-oji is consistently misprinted with an initial lower-case 'l' (pp. 4 *ff.*); then we have 'eduction' for education (p. 5); bookship for bookshop (p. 25); socieities for societies (p. 43); aquisition for acquisition (p. 61); stubborness for stubbornness (p. 65); anti-climatic for anti-climactic (p. 66); incompatability for incompatibility (p. 104). Then there is the unfortunate 'he cannot never see himself' (p. 39), the branding of Bayo as a 'pimp' when the more correct word is 'gigolo' (p. 40), and the inelegance of the stylistic use of 'italics mine' which begins a sentence on page 45. Lastly, one notes the incompleteness of the bibliography and the unorthodoxy of its compilation.

On the positive side – to which most of the rest of this review will be devoted – the author must be congratulated on the thoroughness of his research and on the completeness of his findings. But one must be braced for what seems a rather higher-handed critical judgment of Ekwensi by Emenyonu than anything Lindfors himself (whom Emenyonu had excoriated for saying the same things) could have come up with. In Chapter I, 'Early Writings', consisting of 'Banana Peel', 'The Tinted Scarf', 'Land of Sani', 'The Cup Was Full', and 'Deserter's Dupe', Emenyonu sees 'uncertainties in the direction of the plots'. '[Ekwensi's] facts', he says, 'are sometimes confused and there are places where revision would have improved the stories immensely'. These early stories, according to Emenyonu, 'are not directly related to each other except in the degrees of flatness and looseness of structure which characterize them'. He further sees in these early writings a 'strong didacticism' (an influence on Ekwensi carried over from Igbo oral tradition) which continues in Ekwensi's later fiction, especially a persistent streak of meting out poetic justice: the good in Ekwensi's fiction are consistently rewarded while the bad are relentlessly punished. Furthermore, Emenyonu sees Ekwensi's pen at this early stage as 'very hasty and impatient'. Loose structure, heavy didacticism, inconsistency of setting, swift poetic justice, hasty construction, resort to mechanical resolution of dilemmas, use of gimmicks, lack of careful revision, and plain bad writing are seen as Ekwensi's literary sins at this stage of his writing. If Emenyonu sees 'impressive' style and economy of language by Ekwensi in 'The Cup Was Full', he is quick to point out the careless and hasty ending and the author's conniving at 'the complexities of rapid cultural change' which the story was all about. And what other critics might see as a unifying structural pattern in 'The Banana Peel' – the tripping and falling over banana peels by various characters – is struck down by Emenyonu as an unconvincing vehicle of tragedy in the story and a gimmick that is at once both 'monotonous and an unrealistic exaggeration'.

'People of the City', reads, according to Emenyonu in Chapter II, 'like indictments of city inhabitants', as Ekwensi persists in pointing out 'the revolting social injustices and outrageous immoralities that seem to have become part of their way of life', because, for Ekwensi

> The city is a terribly corrupting influence, a den for Ali Baba where forty thieves have stored all their gold, and anyone who has the magic words can go and help himself. And sometimes greed traps the sesame and the thieves come back and stab the intruder to death as they did to Ali Baba's brother.

Then follows what reads like the author's own indictments of Ekwensi's *People of the City*: swift poetic justice (Beatrice I, 'the hot stuff that Europeans are crazy about', is buried in a pauper's grave, and Aina, the mature teenage prostitute, is stripped naked in public); forced didacticism at the end; weaknesses in character delineation (too many are stereotypes); untidiness in plotting (reads like many smaller stories collected in one book); lack of distance between author (Ekwensi) and his subject matter that causes him to stand in heavy judgment over his 'people of the city', by too strong an insistence on his theme: the wages of sin is death. Emenyonu sees the ending of *People of the City* as both melodramatic and unconvincing, and the whole novel as overcrowded with characters, forcing Ekwensi into the obnoxious habit of killing off characters he has no more use for. In matters of style and rhetoric, the author notes the inelegance with which Ekwensi handles pidgin English at this stage in his writing career, as opposed to his mastery of the same medium in *Jagua Nana*. The heaviest blow on Ekwensi descends in two separate judgments: that '*People of the City* should have been a journalistic documentary on the city instead of an integrated novel about the city', and for those for whom this is still vague, Emenyonu adds: 'The habit of killing off the characters he has no more use for seems indicative of a lack of solid literary talent.' One heaves a sigh of relief that this last comes not from the pen of Lindfors or from the poisoned mind of an 'expatriate'!

What the author sees as strengths in *People of the City* stem not from art but from commitment on Ekwensi's side, not from any literary accomplishment but from Ekwensi's 'great seriousness in dealing with the problems of his society', and from 'the author's effective delineation of the realities of Africa's emerging urban environment'.

In Chapter III, 'Children's Literature', Emenyonu continues to spot weaknesses in Ekwensi, though somewhat tempered and balanced by some emerging strengths: he sees heavy didacticism (*Drummer Boy*); excessive violence (*Yaba Roundabout Murder*); overexcitement over female anatomy plus poor plotting (*Trouble in Form Six*). For a change, much critical praise is meted out for Ekwensi's literary accomplishments. Emenyonu praises the tightly constructed plot and neat resolution of *Drummer Boy*, and he is enthusiastic about the suspenseful narrative and dynamic style of *Passport of Mallam Ilia*. At this point in his work, the author seems to have exhausted his quarry of negative responses and has begun to warm up to his subject.

Chapter IV, 'Collections', is actually out of place. It properly belongs to Chapter I, 'Early Writings'. But Chapter V, '*Jagua Nana*', offers the most perceptive criticism of *Jagua Nana* to appear in print anywhere. *Jagua Nana* is the only work of Ekwensi with which Emenyonu himself is carried away. His enthusiasm for it is palpable; for *Jagua Nana* he has nothing but praise. Since he apparently finds no fault with it, he offers the most in-depth and the most extended analysis of the novel ever – an analysis that really begins with 'Fashion Girl' of the previous chapter, and continues up to Chapter VI. It also seems Emenyonu is at his best when he stops ferreting out deficiencies and bends down to the job of appreciative criticism. He calls *Jagua Nana* 'a different and much better novel than *People of the City*'. He sees in the novel evidence of Ekwensi's maturity and of his 'growing mastery of the novel [form]', especially in his masterful handling of the complex character of Jagua.

Although Emenyonu does not use the term, his study of *Jagua Nana* reveals that Ekwensi was *Henry Jamesian* in his portrayal of Jagua's character: she is the 'central intelligence' through whose eyes the reader perceives other people and events in the novel. And she is also, Jamesian fashion, the centre towards which everything points, and her fate is 'what supremely matters' and structures the novel.

Although in this chapter Emenyonu continues to see weaknesses born out of didacticism and circularity of structure by Ekwensi, he does point to artistic growth in him: mastery of pidgin English in *Jagua Nana*, tighter structure, ability to handle complex characterization, and so on. After this chapter, the rest is anti-climax, as Chapter VI ('*Beautiful Feathers* and *Iska*') and the last chapter ('Conclusion') provide no fresh insights.

Cyprian Ekwensi offers bold insight into certain constants in Ekwensi's canon. For those who like to pick out themes like raisins from a bun, Emenyonu's study of Ekwensi will be most rewarding. When Ekwensi's works are taken together, according to the author, it will be seen that the themes he grapples with include: 'the impact of the forces of inevitable change upon the traditional society'; 'concern for change and an awareness of the impending conflict between the old and the new' ('The Cup Was Full'); 'the rising depravity of the city and its potential [*sic*] destructive influence on young, innocent girls' ('When Love Whispers'); the corrupting influence of the city (*People of the City*); rebellion against the system and a search for identity (*Jagua Nana*).

As the first book-length study of Ekwensi, Emenyonu's *Cyprian Ekwensi* is a bold first: it is complete, thoroughly researched, and will likely remain for a long time the most carefully documented biographical and critical source-book on Ekwensi. Although on the critical balance-sheet Emenyonu's study of Ekwensi is uneven (because of his heavy-handed catalogue of Ekwensi's artistic weaknesses), it is a work that promotes both appreciation and critical evaluation, biographical insights and historically interesting titbits. It is a not-to-be-missed scholarly work for critics, students, and teachers of African literature.

Index

Lightning Source UK Ltd.
Milton Keynes UK
UKOW05f0926040617
302614UK00007B/75/P